Life, Death and Spirituality

Peace and Harmony Without Religion

Richard E. Jensen, PhD, ABPP

Copyright © 2015
Richard E. Jensen, PhD, ABPP
All rights reserved.
Scanning, uploading or distribution of this book via the Internet or any other means without the permission of the publisher is forbidden and punishable under law. Please purchase only authorized electronic editions, and do not participate in or encourage piracy of copyrighted materials. Your support of the author's rights is appreciated.

ISBN-13: 978-1507653661

Well Found Books
wellfoundbooks.com

Dedicated to my wife and Special Susan:

C. Susan Hedke

Acknowledgments

Several reviewers looked at this manuscript in various stages of completion and I am indebted to all of them for their kindness and thoughtfulness in critiquing my draft.

Moderator Richard L. Holinger, PhD and the St. Charles Writers Group (SCWG) provided substantial assistance for this project in the form of critical review. The group, sponsored by the St. Charles Public Library (Illinois), was founded in 1995 by Dr. Hollinger through a START grant. The writers come and go as their projects emerge, develop into maturity and finally to completion. A dynamic core membership provides basis for a cohesive group dedicated to writing in nearly every genre and offering skillful criticism to peers. The mechanics of SCWG are not very different from others that I have experienced but it functions more effectively. I appreciate actionable criticism which provides the writer an opportunity to make changes in the direction of clarity, readability and artistic rendering.

Many thanks to Twila Greenheck for an important review of the manuscript during the time that I was pulling the pieces together.

Special thanks to my wife, C. Susan Hedke, for her reviews, critiques, consultations and for her kind attention to some of my less compelling ideas and formulations. She is the consummate "in-house" reviewer.

Table of contents

Reader Notes xi

Preface xiii

Part 1: Orientation

Chapter 1 Is the News Good or Bad?
Reality is Fine.. 1

Chapter 2 Can I Get There From Here?
Origin and Model.. 13

Chapter 3 Where Should I Stand?
Fulcrum and Leverage... 21

Chapter 4 Could Anything Slow Me Down?
East Meets West... 33

Part 2: Disappointment

Chapter 5 Does it Really Matter?
Life and Death... 43

Chapter 6 Is this Problem Real?
Fear of the Dark and Death Anxiety................................... 49

Part 3: Concepts and Realities

Chapter 7 Wholeness in Skepticism?
Healthy Doubts.. 61

Chapter 8 Does "Spiritual but Not Religious" Really Fit?
SBNG... 73

Chapter 9 Something Magical?
Natural Spirit... 83

Chapter 10 Could We Skip the Smoke and Mirrors?
Realistic Perspective... 91

Chapter 11 True Grit: Magic Too?
Pluck & Rigor..103

Part 4: Methods

Chapter 12 Any Relief from the Stress?
Relaxation... 111

Chapter 13 Do I Need Meditation?
Meditation I.. 119

Chapter 14 Can I Wash this Junk Out of My Head?
Meditation II... 127

Chapter 15 Should I Keep on Scrubbing?
Meditation III.. 135

Chapter 16 Isn't Meditation just Meditation?
Meditation IV.. 145

Chapter 17 How could Meditation Actually Work?
Meditation V... 151

PART 5: Conclusion

Chapter 18 Fearless Being and Becoming?
Oneness... 157

Chapter 19 Can't I Just Have What I Want?
Tolerance and Craving... 167

Chapter 20 Are We Unstoppable Now?
Real Limitations... 177

Chapter 21 From Angst to Acceptance?
A View from the Path... 181

Mini Glossary.. 189

References.. 193

Index.. 203

Reader Notes

Caution

This book is intended as a guide for healthy individuals seeking positive growth toward managing ordinary and expected life problems including religious angst and fear of death.

It is not offered as a substitute for mental health treatment, nor is it intended as a guide for dealing with mental health adjustment problems or severe mental illness.

If you are under treatment or have recently completed treatment with a mental health professional, it is important to consult your specialist about the suitability of the model described here, before going forward.

Point of View

This book is written from the viewpoint of a freethinking Westerner with a keen interest in alternative frames of reference. I do not apologize for the point of view expressed here. Rather, I am advocating for it. I was born, grew up and educated in the US. It's clear to me that the stamp of the US and the Western world is upon me. When I think about faith and religious traditions the, Abrahamic religions are my usual starting place for making comparisons. My worldview is substantially influenced by the research the framework commonly referred to as the scientific method. But, as you will see in the chapter text, there are several other components I advocate to encompass a sufficient worldview. Chapter 10 is the most pointed exposition of this viewpoint.

Style

American Psychological Association Style, APA Style, is generally used by disciplines within the Social Sciences.

Disciplines using APA Style Include but are not limited to:
- Business
- Communication
- Criminology and Criminal Justice
- Education
- Nursing

The major characteristics of APA Style include use of the publication author name and date of publication in parentheses in the body of the text to identify the source. Full bibliographic information for these citations is then listed in a "Reference" section, alphabetically by author last name.

Preface

I grew up un-churched with parents who belonged to a mystical tradition. The instruction they studied was provided in the form of written monographs that members read at home. My Mom espoused substantial interest in the mystical tradition, but did not seem content with it. She was constantly seeking support and comfort for her religious anxieties and hence gravitated to a variety of groups offering hope and consolation. It was clear to me that she had little interest in testing out the validity of her ideas, but rather that she was searching for reassurance. In contrast, my Dad was mechanically inclined and bought the discipline of machinery, logic and language to everything he did. He was not particularly fond of Christian theology and early in his life moved toward a mystical orientation. Mystics believe that they can be in direct contact with the larger forces of the world without the need for a clergy or religious organization as intermediaries. They use meditation as a regular practice to find peace and harmony within themselves. My father seemed to be quite content with the avenues he had found and seem to have few, if any, unmet spiritual needs. Other family members were healthy skeptics. They offered an alternative frame of reference to the Christian worldview and the mystic assertion of an invisible world which they can access through meditation.

As a youngster I was somewhere in between. I was curious about Sunday morning meeting groups (church) and attended some with cousins who seemed to subscribe to their religious practices and theology uncritically. In my undergraduate years I had two courses in theology, Old Testament and New Testament as well as courses in philosophy, one Greek and one modern. I describe my background to caution that my theological / philosophical background is somewhat limited. As an adult I studied clinical psychology completing the usual doctoral program and internship plus a one year fellowship in behavioral therapy. I have served students and patients in my role as a college faculty member and as a clinician in outpatient and inpatient programs in various locations over the years. Hence, I speak with some authority on many issues in psychology.

I have had the opportunity to ponder many of these issues over the years and on occasion have had a chance to talk them through with interested colleagues and scholars. *Life, Death and Spirituality, Finding Peace and Harmony Without Religion* has been germinating since the 1970s. In fairness, the book that I might have written at that time would have gone in a very different direction. Hence, I am reminded of the benefit of turning things over for a while. The experience that suggested that I might still have the fire in my belly to write a book in this area came when I was a participant in a lay led discussion group called, "Building Your Own Theology," at a Unitarian Universalist church group.

I now look forward to sharing this perspective with you.

Chapter 1
Is the News Good or Bad?
Reality is Fine

Overview

We look at fundamental assumptions about human nature and implications of such views for our future. We also preview this book by looking at what this book is and what it is not.

Quotations

Nature has no principles. She makes no distinction between good and evil. *Anatole France*

To prefer evil to good is not in human nature; and when a man is compelled to choose one of two evils, no one will choose the greater when he might have the less. *Plato*

Compassion alone stands apart from the continuous traffic between good and evil proceeding within us. *Eric Hoffer*

The line between good and evil is permeable and almost anyone can be induced to cross it when pressured by situational forces.
Philip Zimbardo

Mysteries do not lose their poetry when solved. Quite to the contrary; the solution often turns out to be more beautiful than the puzzle and, in any case, when you have solved the mystery uncover others, perhaps to inspire greater poetry. *Richard Dawkins*

I still believe, in spite of everything, that people are truly good at heart. *Mark Twain*

Introduction

I am a psychologist (now retired) with considerable interest in life, death, spirituality, peace and harmony. I have rejected magic since my teen years, except for fun shows of sleight-of-hand. As you will see in detail later, since I am careful about magic, the idea of accepting organized religion is a step too far for me. Probably the niche in which I fit best is "freethinker." That is, one who uses the tools of logic and science to find their way. Over the years I have affiliated with Unitarian Universalist fellowships, societies, or churches in my local area at the time. I ask you to join me on a path that will take us toward our own peace and harmony. We will travel together, because I am a seeker, too.

This book deals with problems of living and acceptance of death. It provides knowledge and skill resources needed to come to terms with both life and death. Many people react to the inevitability of death by denying, pretending or minimizing. They may harbor a fantasy that we all live in a world everlasting and that we, too, are everlasting. Reality is quite to the contrary. Once born, we have a 100% chance of dying. The only question is when. The institutional answer to our disappointment is organized religion, prayer, theology, reassurance, and externalizing the problem of death to a distant, idealized and personal God. We all know the truth. This book is based on a simple notion: we can all learn to cope with the issues of living in a natural world in which we die. We can do this in our spare time, as individuals or in instructor-guided classes.

Although narrower in scope, this book is in the tradition of the large questions which have always been relevant to human-kind. For example, the meaning of life, how to live a life, what is truth, where truth and justice lie. This book takes a substantial departure from the supernatural world offered by many world religious traditions and the personal and institutionalized view supported by

Chapter 1 : Is the News Good or Bad?

prayer to an external personal God.

An analysis of the problem is provided together with a path toward a personal solution. The path requires the seeker to do both intellectual and emotional work. We need to understand the problem that is smothering us and we need to equip ourselves for action. The strategies offered for making needed changes include: skepticism, problem analysis, knowledge and understanding, skill development, confronting the realities of the natural world and coming to terms with who we are as people. In addition to conceptual approaches, there are practical remedies incorporated in a methods section. These include; personal growth, refuting obsolete beliefs, relaxation skills and meditation skills. The connection between deep muscle relaxation, meditation and avenues of personal and psychological change are developed.

The reader is invited to become a new person of their own making. This book provides only the opportunity and the means. Readers will need to deliver the motivation, the sustained energy, and the tenacity to make the life changes they wish to achieve.

About the Book Title

If anyone picks up this book based on the title alone, chances are it is comfortable for them. Why, because they are ready to deal with the notion of, "Without Religion." But, of course the question is, why am I so finicky about this? To espouse agnosticism or worse yet, atheism is to potentially alienate a lot of people in the vicinity. Why, because they reject the concept of God in which many people trust and believe. One of the terrible vulnerabilities of being human is, sometimes our most cherished beliefs are held only tenuously and require substantial social support to maintain them. When people speak out in opposition to them we understandably feel a sharp loss of social support for our views. So what am I, some sort of mythic George Washington who cannot tell a lie? I try to say what I mean and mean what you say. But, of course there are times when I bite my tongue, like everyone else with any modicum of social awareness.

We all understand the "God" Vs "No God" argument is historic, controversial and polarizing. But, why take on that baggage here? Because this is a book and you are a reader. Good and new ideas have been discussed in books for centuries. No one will be offended if it turns out this book is not for you, and you simply put it down. As we shall see later, we have to distinguish between the concept of God, and the question of the existence of God. What emerges is, adding the God concept to the discussion of how the natural world actually works is not only cumbersome and not very helpful, but quite misleading. More on this later.

We will make frequent allusions to "nature." This book is not about a repudiation or put-down of anything or anybody. It is an attempt to offer something positive to people who are ready to consider it. The idea of nature does not include anything contrived or supernatural. We know about nature based on our sense experience of the world around us, what we learned in school and also through the common knowledge shared by others in our social world. Sunrise and the daylight go together as do sunset and darkness. The natural world provides us constant opportunities to confirm the basics of how our world functions.

The Good News

Let's clarify some basics. Everyone is born good and can live full, productive and happy lives without fear of sin, Hell, or damnation. We can just go forward with our lives kicking off this excess baggage and making the most of what we have. For those trapped in the belief that everyone is born a sinner and must repent, earn salvation, or purify ourselves, I am here to deliver good news. In this case, the good news is not exactly that Jesus died for our sins, but rather, we weren't born with any sin, original or any other kind.

All humanity, regardless of race, creed, national origin, time of birth, time of death is free to enjoy the same benefits we are. That is, because all of humankind has always been born morally good and we do not need to redeem ourselves from any sort of prejudicial

Chapter 1 : Is the News Good or Bad?

actions of our forbearers. How could this be? There is nothing wrong with being born. The only known way for people to appear on earth, at least before cloning, is to be born to a mother with the genetic assistance of a father, and with the exception of assault, there is nothing wrong with that. Therefore, birth is not a stigmatic or prejudicial status and cannot be the basis of sin. Nor can it be a dishonor by association or by doctrines of some subsequent religious creeds or theologies. So, not even those born before the arrival of what various religions believe to be their savior, cannot be into some kind of disfavor because they were born before the saviors "forgiveness" was given.

In case we're not yet comfortable accepting this world view, we can do something that will help us make a change, such as counter-propagandizing ourselves (Ellis, 1963). For example, we can develop a written list of arguments that refute these disabling ideas we have been carrying around. Make sure your counter arguments are direct and forthright. Or, if that is not suitable, consider the possibility of devising some rite of absolution that will get the job done, like laying your finger on the side of your nose and rising up the chimney or taking a gray-coat along even on a sunny day. Or do whatever else is stylistically suitable. In any case, please waste no more than ten minutes on this. The point is there is no wrong can be righted. Doing something to be absolved is just a little bit of silliness to make ourselves feel better. Hence, any kind of brief conscience palliating activity that will release us is quite sufficient.

Doctrines like sin, Hell and damnation are powerful for those who accept them. The power such notions wield over us depends directly on the power we give to them. That is, unless we provide these ideas with authority over us, they're just floating around without the ability to harm anyone. Once we give them legitimacy and allow them to be real, to guide our thought or action, they may very well have a powerful effect on our attitudes, beliefs, values and, certainly, our behaviors. Together we can find ways to empower ourselves to go forward, to find meaning and value in a world which has dramatically changed since the advent of intimidating religious doctrines.

At the same time, I am not ready to talk anybody into changing their views. My hope is that this book can be a resource for people to make the changes that will work for them in their lives. I have long believed everyone's personal religion is the right thing for them. Yet, if there is opportunity to quiz someone about their religious foundation, including their practice and theology, it soon becomes clear what chafes or rankles them. Many people find themselves in the dilemma of defending their faith to others, but then find themselves stuck with it when it doesn't fit for them anymore. We can make the changes we want and move in whatever direction we choose.

In order to undertake this journey, it will be important to have a high tolerance for ambiguity and uncertainty. A sense of adventure wouldn't hurt either. In this process, it will be important to be thoughtful, deliberative, earnest, hard-working, and open to change. The essence of what is offered here is not much of a mystery, since the clues have been all around us for decades. Still, like all aspirations, hopes, inventories of resources and studies of feasibility, it will take substantial determination to succeed. If we find something new and appropriate for us, we may choose to shed something old to make way for it. This whole proposition is best summed up by saying, there is a premium on ambiguity-tolerance and adventure, and it is not for the faint hearted.

Wait a moment, you say, what about Anatole France, above? You quoted her saying, "Nature has no principles. She makes no distinction between good and evil." Then you tell us that all humanity is born "good." I was just checking to see if you are paying attention. Born "good" or "evil" are value judgments that don't apply in a natural world. All creatures are born into the world. No evaluative judgment can be realistically applied as Anatole France pointed out. But John Calvin (1536) did not agree, "…our nature is not merely bereft of good, but is so productive of every kind of evil. . . ." My

Chapter 1 : Is the News Good or Bad?

excuses are zeal and rhetorical flourish. Look carefully at the function of Calvin's argument. It has the effect of "controlling the flock" by putting us in a one-down position. That is, we are evil, but he can lead the way to help us out of our dreadfulness. This is clearly self-serving for the "Calvins" of the world.

The Bad News

Just like all of the rest of life, there are some things that go together and can't be separated. This bad news isn't all that bad. The story known as, The Devil and Daniel Webster, the movie called, *Rosemary's Baby* and the notion of the Black Mass (invoking the devil) are all fictions. There is no Easter Bunny, or Santa Claus, but, cheer up, I think we're still good on The Great Pumpkin. If the idea is coming through that we need to:

Find ways to make the most of what we have

Come to terms with ourselves and our neighbors

Live in a natural world of scarcity

Work hard to make our way

Resolve misunderstandings within ourselves and with others

. . . , then we are on track.

Here is an important piece of the puzzle that actually makes our task easier. There is no urgency; there is no hurry to move in these directions. Still the question occurs, if it is important to do this, why shouldn't there be time urgency about getting it done? I have to wonder if it's just the opposite. The more we rush anxiously to pursue an urgent change in our being, the more we are likely to get in our own way. There is little need to stress ourselves for the next achievement, or to rush to Heaven or Nirvana, or whatever label is currently fashionable. If we do, we will have done ourselves a disservice. Simply put, we have our lifetimes in which to follow our path.

Consider the metaphor of the dental chair. Would it help any to be in a rush, once you arrived at the dental office, to have the procedure completed? I don't know about you, but for me, the dentist or the assistant, or other office staff takes care of it. The best thing we can do is relax, find our personal harmony, and work with the clinical staff providing the care. It might be a good idea to let-up a little in order to find our peace and harmony. This is not to say we should be passive. To the contrary, we need to be active and persistent, but we also need to relax and savor the journey.

At the same time, finding our path is no substitute for formal education, technical skills, cultural understanding, empathy for others, tolerance, patience, and persistence. We are talking about living a life here, not about finding salvation from some fictional evil. Remember the good news? *Everyone Is Born Good!* Everyone has the chance to make the most of their life situation, his or her person, being, and uniqueness. Even though I have tempered and qualified my remarks on goodness, above, I think these are still reasonable statements to make.

I think it's fair to say that the terms of this transaction are rather different from those offered in the Abrahamic religious traditions. We need to work out our feelings; tolerances and goals for developing a worldview that will help us better understand the larger world. In a very important way, this book is about us, rather than about some distant personal deity.

Chapter 1 : Is the News Good or Bad?

Table 1.1: What this Book Is and What It is Not

What it is	What it is not

A Journey of
    Concern
    Seeking
    Discovery
	A Defamation of any
	    Religion
	    Creed
	    Personal Path

A Search for personal
    Peace
    Harmony
    Wholeness
	A Search for Salvation

A Consideration of Alternatives
    Personal
    Natural
    Ethical
	An Inspired Work
	    It took effort to conceive, plan & write
	    It will almost certainly take effort
	    to understand & apply

A Statement of a
    Conceptual model
    World-view
    Frame of reference
	Part of any movement like
	God Is Dead.
	or ...Alive
	or ...Arriving Any Minute
	or... Out to Lunch, etc.

An approach to Analysis Evaluation	Gratuitous putdown of others
Consideration of alternative life strategies Feasibility assessment Selection	Glib deference to dysfunctional ways of thinking
A Formulation of Who? Where? What? Why? When? How?	An Apology for Anything

Some Religious Trends in the US

How do people handle the prescriptions of their religious faith over time? I have referred to the Calvinist's controlling religious doctrine and alluded to the difficulty of a distant personal God. Institutional religion is at least about beliefs in doctrine and the practice or religious ceremonies. The world has many long standing religious traditions and the US certainly has representatives of many of them. But what is the trend in religious belief and what significance does it have?

The trend is quite clear and powerful. People are turning away from organized religion (cf. NPR, Jan. 13, 2013 f). Are we following the trend in seeking our own path to peace and harmony? Not so much. At least I would not recommend it. In Part 3, Concepts

Chapter 1 : Is the News Good or Bad?

Figure 1.1 General Social Survey

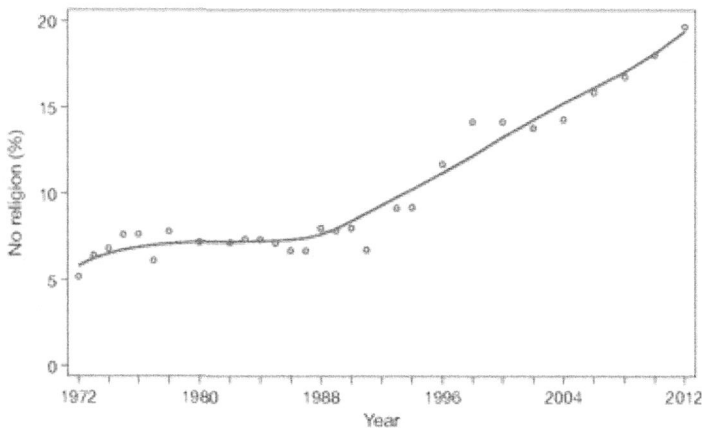

Note: Line smoothes the data to highlight main trend. The circles are each survey's estimate
Source: General Social Surveys. 1972-2012

The General Social Survey has been tracking major social and cultural trends in American society since 1972, when only 5 percent of those polled claimed no religion. Since 1990, an uptick in those identifying themselves as following no particular religion has progressed steadily with 18 percent identifying as such in 2010 and 20 percent in 2012. (Anwar, 2013)

and Realities (Ch. 7 -11) we will look at some criteria for making decisions about what will pay-off for us. In general, following social trends is a tough treadmill and we would want to have something more substantial to navigate our life course than social trends.

Q & A

I guess all we have to do is go forward and we can do this thing. Our lives and our life outcomes will take care of themselves. If I got it right, why would you write this book?

Well, you got it almost right. We do need to go forward with our lives and the decisions we make affect the outcomes we will live with in the future. Nothing takes care of itself and there is no free ride. It takes grit, a term we will fully define shortly.

Haven't you already contradicted yourself? In Table 1.1 you indicate that this book is not a defamation of any religion, creed or personal path and that it is not a gratuitous put-down of others. You seem to already be making value judgments, identifying what works and what does not. How does this square up?

Making our own choices is not a defamation of other philosophical or religious views. We must all find our own way and encourage others to do likewise. Life is about making decisions. Our choices define who we are and which way we are going. Yes, I certainly have made judgments and in this beginning chapter I have shared them with you, my reader. As we will see, there are those who argue that we are condemned to be "free" by the decisions we make (Sartre, Ch. 5). We will also develop the notion of the behavioral analysis (AKA, force field analysis). More later, but for now, behavior analysis a look at where a course of behavior (choices) would likely take us.

Bottom line, what does it take to do this thing? Can it really be so hard?

It will take at least intellectual and emotional work and require persistence. The natural world does not reward us for just making a good try, but we will surely be rewarded for our successes.

Chapter 2
Can I Get There From Here?
Origin and Model

Overview

We look at how people cope with life and death issues and how it is they come to search for peace and harmony. The first section provides a narrative followed by a table summarizing the circumstances in which we may come to this search. Then, bullet point summaries are provided of the major themes of this book.

Quotations

To thine own self be true . . . *William Shakespeare*

Discontent is the first step in the progress of a man or a nation. *Oscar Wilde*

Knowing yourself is the beginning of all wisdom. *Aristotle*

The only journey is the one within. *Rainer Maria Rilke*

And you? When will you begin that long journey into yourself? *Rumi*

No one remains quite what he was when he recognizes himself. *Thomas Mann*

Coming to Our Path

We may arrive at our search from many different directions. We may find ourselves happy, content and free, yet want to move forward toward life's full satisfaction and adventure. We might also start from a stressed, worried, overwrought situation and be eager to resolve our current difficulties. No matter what our starting point, the path to peace and harmony is available to each of us.

Psychologist Abraham Maslow (1954) developed a model of motivation which identified the human ability to move forward to higher levels of functioning, provided our basic requirements are met. He refers to these basic needs as deficiency or deficit needs. Once our physiological and safety needs are met, he proposes we move on to belongingness, self-esteem and self-actualization. Of course, if anything happens to disrupt our life circumstances, like loss of a job or a home, a catastrophic fire or flood, we are back to meeting our physiological needs as a primary focus.

What happens if people are caught in the behavioral trap of severe emotional stress? In general, we react to highly tense situations by seeking fulfillment of only deficiency needs. We may find ourselves reacting with substantial apprehension and anxiety. In such situations we are likely to feel stressed, edgy, worried, demoralized and overwrought. Our reaction to this kind of emotional trap is likely to produce ineffective coping responses that only make our situation worse. We might find ourselves craving, grasping, and clutching for others in search of support, assistance, consolation, sympathy, reassurance or guarantees that we will be OK, while we actually feel overwhelmed. That is, when we are caught in a behavioral trap we often lose our basic coping strategies and no longer solve our immediate or long term problems (cf. Elliot and Smith, 2003), but search for emotional support. This is a downward spiral.

If we are fortunate enough to meet our basic needs and move forward to the domain of growth needs, we may be able to let go, release ourselves from behavioral traps and instead experience the freedom of growing and moving forward. We might do this in the

Chapter 2 : Can I Get There From Here?

form of celebrating our gifts, feeling a sense of increased confidence, experiencing increased capability to tolerate uncertainty, being interested in new challenges and taking comfort in our successes with increased self-confidence. We may be able to benefit sufficiently to move forward to a more intuitive approach to the problems that surround us. Perhaps we can adopt more rational and logical cognitive approaches, seek out the problems and formulate solutions to them, become increasingly functional in our world and in enhancing our personal growth. We are now good candidates for life's adventure toward peace and harmony. We may be able to find simplicity, contentment, new directions, increasing productivity, meaningfulness, understanding, joy, blossoming, and ultimately the goal of peace and harmony. This is an upward spiral.

The table below visualizations and summarizes these personal needs and sequences them in a progressive fashion to identify that, as we achieve satisfaction of each level of needs, we are positioned to move forward to higher levels of functioning.

Table 2.1 Finding Your Path

Anxiety, Apprehension Existential Angst	Craving, Grasping, Clutching	Letting Go, Releasing, Freeing	Moving Forward	Life's Adventure

Deficiency Needs   **Growth Needs**

Stressed, Edgy, Tense	Support	Celebration of gifts	Intuitive	Simplicity
Worried	Aid, Assistance	Confidence	Rational, Logical	Contentment
Overwrought	Consolation, Sympathy	Ambiguity tolerance	Problem seeking	New directions
Low ambiguity tolerance	Reassurance	New challenges	Problem solving	Productivity
Loss of concentration	Guarantees	Self-acceptance	Functionality	Meaningfulness
Pressed, Besieged			Growth, Development	Understanding
Demoralized				Recreation
Overwhelmed				Joy
				Blossoming

Chapter 2 : Can I Get There From Here?

Line of Argument of this Book
- The substantial challenges of living and the risks of life and death may become a heavy burden for any of us.
- The fundamental disappointments of uncertainty and death may produce denial, minimizing, and pretense that all is well.
- People may be distressed by life choices and decisions and the less than positive outcomes in navigating difficult situations.
- Sometimes people become unduly focused on the potential for bad outcomes (Catastrophes).
- The stresses that individuals face and their responses to them, including highly effective coping behavior, as well as depression, anxiety and existential angst are important concerns.
- Difficulty in coping with life problems and concerns about end-of-life problems are real and need to be recognized and addressed.

Life Perils Giving Rise to the Model

Here is a starter set for the model that is framed below. It is intended as a "warm-up" or orientation.
- Sometimes we fill our lives with needless torment and suffering of our own making.
- We may unknowingly fall into a behavioral trap.
- Much of our stress or suffering comes from craving what we don't have.
- If we can diminish or preclude craving, we may be able to move on to:
    - Peace
    - Harmony

Cautions
- It takes grit.
- There is no magic.

Conceptual Model

- The childhood fear of the dark is a simple metaphor and model of life anxiety and death anxiety. In the same way that youngsters are helped by parental coaching, the rest of us may be able to find ways to deal with the ongoing life stressors, as well as concerns about death.
- Institutionalized religion provides answers for some life challenges and problems, but these solutions are characteristically not based on valid observation or logical inference. Such world views rely on faith and a belief in a supernatural power to sustain them.
- A naturalistic worldview offers an alternative. Skepticism, questioning, and the search for evidence-based and logically developed understandings provide an alternative and possible remedy.
- Our search for the path to peace and harmony is based in the observable, natural world. No superstition or magic is needed to sustain this model.
- Rigorous thinking, experiential learning, persistence, resilience and vigor, will be required to find and follow our path.
- Personal grit can be discovered within ourselves by managing physical and mental resources.
- Methods used to accomplish these goals include powerful techniques adapted to our needs:
    - Increased conceptual understanding
    - A brief, efficient and powerful relaxation exercise
    - A modified form of ancient meditation techniques
- Personal oneness and wholeness is our objective rather than fearlessness
- Both mindfulness and personal reflection are benefits of starting on our path to peace and harmony.
- With increased understanding, alternative frames of reference and grit, but no magic, we have an excellent chance of finding our path to peace and harmony.

Chapter 2 : Can I Get There From Here?

Advocacy

It is not my goal to write a dispassionate analysis of the problems presented by the topics discussed here, or to pronounce that all world views provide an equal opportunity to understand the realities of our situation. I am clearly an advocate of personal growth and of coming to terms with ourselves in the form of peace and harmony. On the question of what kind of a world view it takes to get an accurate understanding of our situation I am no less and advocate. We will dialogue our way through the issues and you will need to be the judge of what is workable for you. As identified in Table 1.1, I see this book as an offer of empowerment, not a prescription.

As you will see in chapter 8, I regard myself as a spiritual person (SPNG) as long as I am permitted to define the kind of spirituality I favor. Why spiritual? (See: Mini- Glossary) Why not agnostic, atheist, theist, deist, or any of the rest of the available classifications? As we will soon see, my definition of spirituality takes considerable exception to the common definitions, and it suits me just fine.

Q & A

Maslow's hierarchy of needs is typically presented as a pyramid. Where's your pyramid? In your table you left out physiological and safety needs altogether, how does this work?

The influence of Maslow's needs hierarchy powerfully affects a lot of people who have taken psychology courses. My point here isn't to replicate Maslow's model, but to identify that it is probably implicit in the thinking of all of us

Could I be starting my search for a path in the wrong way? If I get off on the wrong foot, can I ever recover?

There's no right or wrong place to start. We'll need to start from where we are and that place is just fine until we are ready to move on to something more workable.

We won't be able to do very much wrong in starting toward or following our personal path.

Are you really saying we don't have to be exceptionally good or special but also, that we don't have to be incurably bad to search for our own path? Is it really OK to be just ordinary people looking for a better life?

Yes. There are no special qualifications required to seek your own path.

Chapter 3
Where Should I Stand?
Fulcrum and Leverage

Overview

We look at a few of the timeless questions about human existence as a way of finding a starting point for our path. We examine long standing ideas of a major wisdom tradition for their relevance to our situation and explore a major critique of an important model. Behavioral and emotional self-regulation provide additional understandability to some apparently conflicting facts.

Quotations

To keep the body in good health is a duty – otherwise we shall not be able to keep our mind strong and clear. *Buddha*

Wealth consists not in having great possessions, but in having few wants. *Epictetus*

Contentment is natural wealth, luxury is artificial poverty. *Socrates*

There are two things to aim at in life: first, to get what you want; and after that, to enjoy it. Only the wisest of mankind achieve the second. *Logan Pearsall Smith*

Figure 3.1: Archimedes Moving Earth

Give me but one firm spot on which to stand, and I will move the earth. *Archimedes*

The Good Life: Prescribed or Self-Determined?

There are many versions of the eternal philosophy-of-life questions. How to best live a life often finishes high on the list. A helpful list can be found at www.psycanics.org. In order to get perspective on our situation, here is a short list:

Who am I?
Why am I here?
How shall I live?
What is happiness?

These are profound questions because they are both intensely personal and highly complex. If the focus of concern is outside ourselves, observation and analysis of what we see, hear, or otherwise discern is a first step. If the concern is some sort of interinal or foundational understanding, we need a starting place. The historic practice would seem to be, go away for a period of time to seek an

Chapter 3 : Where Should I Stand?

inspirational vision by altering our state of consciousness. Then, return with the good news of triumph. But, starting from where? The choices would seem to be:

> Normal work-a-day
> Self-indulgence
> Ascetic, self-denial

We look at each of these alternatives to see if they offer clues about where to go next.

The normal, work-a-day life of every day routine seems unlikely to inspire us to anything different. For example, if you have ever had to sweep or hose off the sidewalk in front of your house, or bail water out of the basement, or any of the many other creature chores that confront us, it will often be hard to remember if you completed a particular part of the task, because it is so routine. No, not very inspiring, not much fun, and these chores offer little novelty or stimulation to change our consciousness. It seems unlikely a break-through inspiration will come from daily chores or work.

At first blush, self-indulgence seems like a good choice. "Wine, women and song" seem to have captured the imagination of men. But what about the nagging back page or even front page news stories about politicians or celebrities who are involved in unsavory actions and fall into disgrace? For example, in Illinois one former governor has served his prison time and is in a rehabilitation program and another remains in prison (Ryan and Blagojevich). Overreaching and self-indulgence seem to be a notorious hazard of living but there is little evidence it leads to wisdom or enlightenment, rather to the contrary.

The common dictionary definition of an ascetic is a person who renounces material comforts and leads a life of austere self-discipline, especially as an act of religious devotion (cf. Dictionary.com). But it quickly takes on additional meanings. In the excerpt below, note the quotes of another source:

"Asceticism means the liberation of the human person," states the Russian Orthodox philosopher Nicolas Berdyaev (1873-1948). He defines asceticism as "a concentration of inner forces and command of oneself," and he insists: "Our human dignity is related to this." Asceticism, that is to say, leads us to self-mastery and enables us to fulfill the purpose that we have set for ourselves, whatever that may be. A certain measure of ascetic self-denial is thus a necessary element in all that we undertake, whether in athletics or in politics, in scholarly research or in prayer. Without this ascetic concentration of effort we are at the mercy of exterior forces, or of our own emotions and moods; we are reacting rather than acting. Only the ascetic is inwardly free. (Ware, 2013).

Self-denial is given a psychological and spiritual significance that appears to have been a chosen path for seekers in the past.

Like Archimedes, we are looking for leverage and a place to stand. The skills of relaxation and meditation will be developed later (Ch. 11 - 15), but at this point it seems important to determine whether our goal of finding peace and harmony is achievable. We borrow liberally from the Buddhists who have a long tradition of thought and wisdom. After developing the notion of relaxation as a stepping stone, we will carefully explore meditation as a method of self-mastery and personal peace. But it is important to know that here, as everywhere else, there are critics who raise important questions. I perceive the Buddhist's model for seeking awakening as well worked out, but it is always worthwhile to look at the arguments of the detractors.

The Buddhists, Considered and Reconsidered

Here is a very brief summary of basic Buddhist principles:

> Life is (can be) frustrating and painful
> Suffering has a cause
> [The cause of suffering can be ended]
> The way or path to end the cause of suffering… is meditation

Chapter 3 : Where Should I Stand?

...

> Excerpted and adapted from The Four Noble Truths of Buddhism, *A Basic Buddhism Guide: Introduction to Buddhism*, 2012.

There is much more to Buddhism than intimated here. But, for now, among many other goals, the Buddhists advocate an altered state of consciousness called Nirvana. It is described in many ways including a deep peace and expansiveness of the mind (Nirvana, 2013). But more importantly, they offer an adaptable technology that we can use to find our path to peace and harmony. Let's look at a significant criticism to see if we can still reasonably pursue this line of thinking:

> From one perspective, Nirvana appears to be the ultimate solution to the problem of life's meaning. Once the "I" is removed from the equation, there is nothing left to experience life's misery. There are questions about this solution, though, which Buddhists themselves are quick to raise. First, to truly extinguish my identity, don't I have to be dead? As long as I remain alive, I will always be experiencing my self-identity. It seems strange to say that the goal of life is to be completely annihilated through death. Second, while most Buddhists feel that Nirvana can be achieved while we are still alive, the concept of nirvana-in-this-life is almost impossible to describe, and very difficult to achieve (Fieser, 2008, Ch. 1, p 6).

Fieser goes on to say:
> In short, Nirvana is shrouded in mystery, and the best I can do is follow the recommended paths for achieving it, while closing my eyes to what Nirvana actually is. While nirvana might be an effective solution to the problem of life's meaning, it is difficult for us to examine this possibility when we can't easily put it into words (Fieser, 2008, Ch. 1, p 6).

I will respond to these concerns, but I hope not object too strenuously:

We need not pursue Nirvana to use meditation as a method for our own purpose of coping with the fears of life and death. Meditation is an important tool we can make use of. It is soothing and clarifying and brings many benefits.

We do not need to "extinguish ourselves" in the service of our goals of peace and harmony, in part because they are more limited than the Buddhist goal of Nirvana. We have a much better chance of finding ourselves by clearing some of the "junk" out of our heads than losing ourselves in an exotic place.

Finally, while Nirvana may be mysterious, the positive benefits of meditation itself are not very mysterious, as briefly described above and in more detail in Chapters 12- 14. (cf. Cahn, & Cahn. 2006).

Self-Regulation

We have been looking for a starting place (a place to stand) in our search for our path to peace and harmony. What we have called normal, self-indulgence and ascetic self-denial don't look very promising, but there are more facts to consider. In psychology, the tendency to seek outside stimulation is referred to as "sensation seeking" and is a personality trait. Individual personal characteristics or qualities are identified by use of common adjectives like decisive, determined, diligent or diplomatic (trait theory, 2013). In the same way that people are high or low in diligence they may be high or low in sensation seeking, optimizing the amount of external stimulation they experience in their lives. Hence, it is worthwhile to take a second look at anything having to do with how we regulate our preferred stimulus level as we go through our daily routines. From this vantage point, the styles of stimulus regulation we have called normal, self-indulgence and ascetic self-denial might be seen differently and rendered as follows:

Chapter 3 : Where Should I Stand?

Deprivation (Self-denial, fasting, chastity)
Novelty (A walk around the block, getting together with friends, a trip to a museum)
Bombardment-Intense sensation seeking (Sex, drugs & rock and roll)

In our daily lives we might have "high-test" coffee in the morning to get started, but switch to decaffeinated by supper time and finish the day drinking warm milk with honey to settle down. Consider a continuum with high level sensation seekers who get involved in extreme sports like auto racing, sky diving and bungee jumping to experience the adrenalin surge. On the other hand, consider the low sensation seekers who are cautious, prudent, careful people who minimize the excitement in their lives. They might drive an economy car on predictably-safe roadways, fly only the safest airlines, but only when needed and use bridges only to cross the river. It is the high sensation seekers who might be able to alter their state of consciousness with their physically and emotionally stimulating activities, but only if they were able to experience the increased stimulus intensity they achieve without jumping off another bridge or out of an airplane with a fast descent, sport parachute.

Of course, the problem for the high sensation seekers is that they seem to have difficulty tolerating a reduction in their stimulus rush. Sensation seeking is a full time job. They must go on to the next tear, in an almost addictive fashion (Roberti, 2004).

Moderation

Not surprisingly, extremes of anything do not seem to help many of us. So, how do we get out of the ordinary, alter our consciousness or become fully awakened? We need to be kind to both our body and our mind. Stress and fatigue are not our friends. Balanced meals, fresh air and exercise have not gone out of style.

The choices considered above can be reframed in light of an understanding of sensation-seeking as a personality trait. In particular the need to regulate our external stimulation in a manner that suits us. So we might start from the earlier list, reproduced below:

> Normal (work-a-day)
> Self-indulgence
> Ascetic self- denial

Weekends may not be the most convenient time for self-denial.

A more accurate depiction of what people typically do in the course of their lives as the example of using hot, high caffeine coffee in the morning and warm milk and honey at the end of the day. In the same manner, we may also adjust our stimulus level to fit our cycle of weekly activities. Hence, incorporating the models of sensation seeking and ongoing behavioral and emotional management, the model looks more like this:

> Deprivation (Self-denial, fasting, chastity)
> Novelty (A walk around the block, getting together with friends, a trip to a museum)
> Bombardment-Intense sensation seeking (Sex, drugs & rock and roll)

Our taste for hyper-stimulation is likely to vary with age; older people tend to be a bit more sedate. Instead of swimming, water skiing and beach volleyball all day, looking at the lake and the scenery may be sufficient for many seniors.

Now it is time to take an additional step. The story of the Buddha seeking enlightenment and awakening tells of his struggles with self-indulgence and ascetic self-denial. It describes his conclusion that neither provided an avenue to his goal of enlightenment. He used what he called "the middle way" or "the middle path" (What Is The Middle Way, 2013). Given this background we would want to reformulate our model for a final time, as follows:

Chapter 3 : Where Should I Stand?

Self-indulgence
The middle way
Ascetic self- denial

In the Buddhist tradition, there is further enriching meaning to be applied here:

In the broadest sense, the Middle Way refers to the correct view of life that the Buddha teaches, and to the actions or attitudes that will create happiness for oneself and others. Thus, Buddhism itself is sometimes referred to as "the Middle Way," indicating a transcendence and reconciliation of the extremes of opposing views. (The Middle Way. 2013)

For Buddhists, the Middle Way refers to both adjusting our stimulation levels to avoid excess, but also to live in a way that reconciles the many contradictions and opposites we experience in our lives. Not to worry, there is no required sign-up to become a Buddhist on the agenda here, but this background will be very useful to us.

Self-Determined, Regulated Moderation

We have our starting place and we can make our own personal choices about how we want to proceed in our lives. We can take good care of our health in the process and regulate our stimulus levels to maximize our comfort levels and our ability to tune-in to ourselves. There is no need to fall into line with some long standing tradition or someone else's prescription.

We may do whatever we want, as long as we recognize that we will need to accept the consequences of our actions. If the consequences are natural, not supernatural, we will be just fine. It is helpful to have both novelty and constancy in our lives. One gets us going and the other helps us feel stable and secure. But, quiet self-reflection seldom hurts. Within our abundance of novelty and quietude we can look within to wash the "junk" out of our heads and sort out our personal issues. We will look at strategies for doing so in later chapters (Ch. 10 -15). In the mean-time, we will examine some of the disappointments of life and consider some helpful concepts and realities that can move us along toward both coping with everyday life and the long term goals of peace and harmony.

Q & A

Why derive your approach from the Buddha? Are you a Buddhist? Is this book some sort of retread of Buddhism?

Buddhism has many traditions, but the Buddha himself (Siddhattha Gotama) did not invoke a deity or other kind of magical thinking to support his world view. He relied on observation, logic and judgment. I am not a Buddhist, but find their insights to be very helpful. I understand the concern about reworking old ideas, but there are some really good ones out there. Ambrose Bierce said it best, "There is nothing new under the sun, but there are lots of old things we don't know."

Unless I'm reading this wrong, you're asking us to start in the same place that the Buddha started. What do you mean we don't have to follow any ancient tradition and that we can do things just the way we want?

You're quite right, in part. We start where the Buddha started, but not without good reason. In addition to his wisdom that has endured a few thousand years, he had good common sense. We cannot expect to abuse our minds or bodies and have them last very long. Armed with concepts like emotional self-regulation we can proceed with eyes wide open to find our path.

Isn't it a little brash and insensitive to apply concepts like sensation seeking to long practiced methods for seeking wisdom?

Gratefully, research and discovery continue. Understanding that we all regulate our stimulus levels all the time helps to put self-indulgence and self- denial into a broad perspective. These are not

Chapter 3 : Where Should I Stand?

anomalies, but a part of the spectrum of every-day life.

What if we routinely seek more novelty or sensation than we think is good for us? How could we cut down?

We can run from ourselves, but we cannot hide. Where ever we go, we are always there. But, we can still manage to move by stepping stones from where we are to another behavioral style or way of being, by tiny steps. For example, we can exercise some weight control by cutting down our portions. Monitoring our own behavior is a good first step. Once we are aware of our behavior, the possibility of change becomes real.

Life, Death and Spirituality

Chapter 4
Could Anything Slow Me Down?
East Meets West

Overview

We look at how cultural perspectives might affect our understanding of the world around us and how this might make understanding our world more difficult.

Quotations

Death, the only immortal who treats us all alike, whose pity and whose peace and whose refuge are for all- the soiled and the pure, the rich and the poor, the loved and the unloved. *Mark Twain*

Death may be the greatest of all human blessings. *Socrates*
No one knows whether death, which people fear to be the greatest evil, may not be the greatest good. *Plato*

Death is for many of us the gate of hell; but we are inside on the way out, not outside on the way in. *George Bernard Shaw*

It is not death that a man should fear, but he should fear never beginning to live. *Marcus Aurelius*

Gods always behave like the people who created them. *Zora Neale Hurston*

East -West Cultural Views

Our cultural experience has a substantial impact on how we perceive the world we live in.

I grew up in Western culture and in the US and I can see I live in just one small neighborhood of a vast metropolis. Over the years the impact has been humbling and I am grateful for the perspective of a larger world. As we will see below, Eastern thought begins form a different place, is rendered differently and has a different focus from Western thought. A summary table is provided below.

Table 4.1:
East and West- Life Philosophies, Religions and Cultural Values

East	West
Hinduism, Buddhism, Confucianism, Taoism	The Abrahamic religions, Greek philosophy

Reality and Truth

Monism- Only one kind of reality.	Dualism- Two kinds of reality- Material and non-material.
Systemic approach- all events in the universe are interconnected.	Individual approach- events and the role of the person.
Become a part of the universe through meditation and right living.	Search outside yourself- Scholarship and research.
Questions about the beginning and end of the universe are not informative.	

Nature of the Divine

Any higher power is immanent in the world, not separate. Within Buddhism, there are no words for the Divine.	The Divine is transcendent, essentially different from creation. Father Imagery is common.
Change is considered an integral part of the world.	Change is associated with degradation and disintegration (As in Plato), especially of the body.
Change does not indicate an inferior or degraded status.	Perfect things, e.g., God, are changeless, immutable.

Enlightenment

Awakening is a major goal. The source of enlightenment and liberation is within the individual.	Prophets, Popes, mullahs and priests convey God's word to ordinary people. Exception: Quakerism (Protestant) emphasizes looking within.
There are many paths to enlightenment.	There is a single path to God and Heaven.

Life, Death and Spirituality

Human Nature

The human body is an illusion and is a distraction, but is not inherently bad.	The human body is seen as a major source of temptation, sin, change and decay. It is a source of ambivalence.

Life and Death

The goal of the afterlife is release from ignorance.	The goal of the afterlife is release from the body and to join with others in the presence of the Divinity.
The ultimate goal is loss of self and merger with the universe.	The self remains the same self throughout eternity.

Individualism / Collectivism

A human being is an integral part of the universe and the society. People are fundamentally connected. Duty towards all others is an important matter.	A human being has an individualistic nature and is an independent part of the universe and the society.
Collectivism is stronger.	Individualism is stronger.

Development / Progress

Cyclic development, hence improvement is a never ending journey.	Linear development, hence improvement has a goal. Development stops when the goal is reached.

Excerpted and adapted from:
LaFave, Sandra (2004) Comparing Eastern and Western Religions. Retrieved February 18, 2013 from: http://instruct.westvalley.edu/lafave/east_west.html
http://www.1world1way.com/coach/cultures_east_vs_west.html

Chapter 4 : Could Anything Slow Me Down?

Understanding Cultural Impact

The analysis that follows is necessarily an oversimplification and is based on polar extremes of each position. In looking at the comparisons below, keep in mind the stated qualities are reasonably accurate, but not precise. As with any generalized analysis, there are exceptions. Eastern religions and cultural refer to Hinduism, and Buddhism, Confucianism and Taoism. Western philosophies and religions refer to the Abrahamic and Greek traditions.

The East offers the notion of monism, with a single kind of reality incorporated into a systemic view. Monism means that we don't have to struggle with a more complex dual reality to figure out which one operates at any given moment. A systems model helps us look at the interrelationship between compartments of the physical or social world or the universe, for that matter. We as individuals are offered a place in the universe, but there are contemplative practices like meditation required to get there. Especially for the Buddhists, questions about the beginning and end of the world are not regarded as informative. This is because they are beyond the scope of our lives and hence do not help us find our way in this world. Of course the rules are a bit different for astronomers equipped with research models and tools to test them.

The West offers a dualistic world view in which there are two realities, the secular and the sacred. Perhaps it is this distinction that brings an expectation of a real distinction between the profane and the sacred. The Western view also places a higher premium on the individual person and hence encourages analysis and research outside of the self. The value of these activities has been demonstrated in the emergence of scholarly research and again in scientific discovery. It incorporates an eschatological worldview in which the expectation is of progress toward an ending pre-defined by God.

In Eastern thinking, any higher power is imminent in the world, meaning that it is right here with us and does not have a separate or transcendent existence. By implication, a higher power is within us as human beings. The lack of words identifying a divine helps to indicate that little or no distinction is made between the natural world and cosmic powers. Change is understood as a continuous, natural process that is expected, and is not regarded as any kind of decay or degradation.

In the West, the Divine is seen as transcendent and different from the natural world. It has a sacred, holy and changeless quality that transcends the natural world. Change is seen to be in the direction of degradation, disintegration, and dysfunction, while progress is seen as moving toward a predefined goal. God is seen as changeless, immutable, transcendent, omniscient and omnipotent.

The East understands human nature as ignorant and in need of enlightenment. Awakening is a major life goal. The source of understanding is within us and seekers are encouraged to pursue it within themselves. The human body is seen as illusion and distraction in the sense that the major focus of existence is our inner life. There is nothing inherently bad about the body, but it is recognized as a diversion from the major goal of enlightenment.

In the West, human nature is seen as sinful and the body is identified as a major focus of base impulses. The body is a source of temptation and decay and is regarded as something that needs to be controlled.

In the Eastern perspective, the source of enlightenment is within the individual. There are masters and enlightened ones to set us on the right course, but we are encouraged to seek a better understanding within ourselves, based on our experience and reason. Spiritual practice is focused on quieting the mind in order for our own light to come from within. There are many paths to enlightenment; each individual needs to walk their own path.

In the West, holy men guide ordinary people to the light. Knowledge, wisdom and enlightenment are perceived to hold authority and are not vested in ordinary people. There is a major emphasis on spiritual practice to develop a personal relationship with a supernatural God. The Society of Friends, Quakerism, is an exception, focusing on searching within and offering testimonies in their otherwise silent meetings.

From the Eastern view, the purpose of life is purification of the consciousness and release from ignorance. The ultimate goal is the loss of self and merger with the universe.

In the West, the afterlife occurs in heaven, a place of reward for good deeds and release form the body. The self remains constant through eternity. However, going to heaven is only for the select. Purgatory and Hell may be the destination of those who fail to reach the goals set by God.

Collectivism is stronger in the East. The human being is seen as part of the community and is fundamentally connected. In the East, development is seen as occurring in cycles, hence improvement is an on-going journey toward Nirvana.

As noted above individualism is stronger in the West and Humans are seen as an independent part of the universe and society. Development is seen as linear, hence improvement has a goal and an end. Development stops when the goal is reached. This is consistent with the eschatological outlook in which all comes to an end.

The table below provides a comparison of the polar extremes of spirituality and religion. As in all such comparisons it is a simplification and there are always exceptions.

Interpretation

Do these cultural world views have any identifiable advantages and disadvantages? They provide different opportunities for understanding the experience of the world around us. We need to understand the differences in cultural views and the implications of those differences to understand the ideas offered by thinkers of different traditions.

The caution is, we have already dramatically simplified the issues we have reviewed and now to further distill an interpretation runs greater risk of error and trivializing the results. Why? Because each time we reduce the data we look at, we lose information. Below, East and West are reduced to six lines each. Editing down to zero words each would really simplify a lot more, but then our summary would deal with no questions or issues at all. The focus here is to try to address the challenges faced by modern seekers on their path to peace and harmony.

East
Fosters a systemic and inward search
Seeks to become one with the universe
Awakening
Recognizes many paths
No proof is expected for personal discoveries
Postulates order and oneness

West
Encourages an individual and outward search
Seeks to know God
Obedience
Follows a single path to God and Heaven
Arguments are subject to test or proof
Scholarship and research

What Could Slow Us Down?

As we have seen, the way we look at the world affects how we respond to it. Cultural views and world-views may allow us to perceive particular subtleties while masking others. We will need to position ourselves to move between differing world views without losing perspective. We are dealing with a problem that is much more challenging then converting weights and measures from one system to another. Because of the fundamental assumptions underlying these worldviews, they reflect importantly different realities that may or may not be accurate.

We need to be increasingly nimble in moving between these worldviews and the constructions they portray, so that we will be able to go forward more easily to find our own peace and harmony.

Chapter 4 : Could Anything Slow Me Down?

Q & A

You provide an interpretation of East and West. Is this the only one?

What we have considered here is a "functional analysis" of two major conceptions of the world. A functional analysis gets at issues like, "What happens if you apply these ideas in the world we live in?" There are many others who speak to these issues and surely I bring my own bias to the task. It seems unlikely that this is that last word on the subject.

Even if we accept this functional analysis of the Eastern and Western worldview, isn't it a little like comparing apples and oranges? Aren't they really different and virtually incomparable?

Bingo, you've got it! They are so different that we might not notice that our worldview is affected by the culture in which we live. We look at these issues so we might get a glimmer of understanding of the blinders we are wearing as we look at the larger world around us.

Chapter 5
Does it Really Matter?
Life and Death

Overview

We look at the human condition and how it is interpreted by a major existentialist and take a personal look at death phobia. Then we compare world views from naturalistic and supernatural perspectives to see where it might take us.

Quotations

Courage is resistance to fear, mastery of fear, not absence of fear. *Mark Twain*

If we don't know life, how can we know death? *Confucius*

Death gives meaning to our lives. It gives importance and value to time. Time would become meaningless if there were too much of it. *Ray Kurzweil*

Life and death are one thread, the same line viewed from different sides. *Lao Tzu*

It is said that men may not be the dreams of the Gods, but rather that the Gods are the dreams of men. *Carl Sagan*

I distrust those people who know so well what God wants them to do because I notice it always coincides with their own desires. *Susan B. Anthony*

The Human Condition

Perhaps the greatest human disappointment is, in the end we all die. This may fill us with denial pretending and minimizing. In all of recorded history, nobody has been able to do anything about it. The institutional answer to our disappointment is organized religion, prayer, theology, reassurance, and externalizing the problem of death to a hoped-for God.

We as individuals, one at a time, need to come to terms with the realities of the natural world in which we both live and die. This is a departure from the supernatural world offered by organized religion and the personal, as well as institutionalized, denial, pretending and minimizing supported by prayer to an external, personal God.

In a chapter called, Death and Immortality: How Do We Celebrate Life? Gilbert (2005) puts it very succinctly:

> Only two problems really exist, and neither one can be solved. One of them is life. And the other is death. (p. 62)
>
> Our mortality is tenuous. We are but guests of existence, brief visitors upon this earth. Many of us are agnostic about immortality. We do not know. We try not to be in denial about our mortality. (p. 64)

"What could be the problem about living?" is the obvious question. Ever run into life challenges, quandaries, problems that needed to be solved? Table 2.1 describes the dilemma of people finding themselves depressed, demoralized and over-whelmed in

Chapter 5 : Does it Really Matter?

their daily lives. This is a circumstance in which we have anxiety, apprehension, or existential angst about our life situation. Søren Kierkegaard (1844 / 1980) is the historical figure who offered the notion that, to follow the Christian faith, we would have to take a "leap of faith" because of the theology has internal contradictions. I don't recommend it, but rather think that we should be seeking peace and harmony. Kierkegaard may have been the first to raise these issues, but he was certainly not the last.

So, there is this problem about life and death. Yes, we can sense, intuit, feel that "death" is a problem, right away. But, as Kierkegaard observed, so is life. Jean Paul Sartre, as we will see in the excerpt below, states, "The individual creates themselves by making self-directed choices," and "As human existence is self-conscious without being pre-defined, we, as autonomous beings, are "condemned to be free. . . ." (Jones, 2012). Yes, there are risks to living and some people struggle with the hazards and need to find their own path. Here is the larger excerpt:

> Jean Paul Sartre was one of the leaders of the French post war left wing intellectual movement, co-founding with Maurice Merleau-Ponty (1908-61) the journal Les Temps Moderns. His experiences as a resistance fighter shaped his philosophy that was influenced by the ideas of Husserl and Heidegger. Politically Sartre claimed he was a Marxist and thought that freedom had both political and individual dimensions.
>
> Unlike Kierkegaard, Sartre was an atheist. As God does not exist, there are no 'essences'. By essence, Sartre is talking about a pre-defined human nature. What Sartre meant by the phrase 'existence precedes essence' is this: If there is no cosmic designer, then there is no design or essence of human nature. Human existence or being differs from the being of objects in that the human being is self-conscious. This self-consciousness also gives the human

subject the opportunity to define itself. The individual creates his/her self by making self-directed choices. As human existence is self-conscious without being pre-defined, we, as autonomous beings are "condemned to be free:" compelled to make future directed choices. These choices induce anxiety and uncertainty into our psyches. If we, as individuals, simply follow custom or social expectations in order to escape this angst, we have escaped the responsibility of making our own choices, of creating our own essence. We have acted in bad faith.

Death Phobia?

There is little wonder I have some reservations about dying, since this life is all I know. When I was about 10 years old my Dad raised the issues of being caretakers for the earth. He observed that we are impermanent, temporary, noting that, we come and we go. For my father these issues were easily confronted and discussed.

This book does not emerge out of my fear of death, but rather my attempt to offer something in the way of a look at the problem and some beginnings of a solution. I am not fearful about death, but I'm also aware that I am not entirely bulletproof about it either. Even though I've had a few decades to entertain these questions, I find that they are still quite poignant. And so, I do still ask myself, how ready am I to deal with the ultimate questions. My guess is that none of us will really know until we get there. This is part of why, together with you I join as a seeker of the path to peace and harmony.

World Views

Let's look a little bit more formally at our perspective on life. That is, how do we view it, or understand it? Just to sharpen up the discussion, Table 5.1 provides a contrast of these views. For the sake of discussion the table provides generalized and poplar extremes of

Chapter 5 : Does it Really Matter?

each view. There are always exceptions.

Table 5.1 Natural World and Supernatural World

Natural World	**Supernatural World**

Living in a brief bubble that might:
    Sag down to a slow collapse
    Burst dramatically and suddenly
	Recipients of a personal gift from a Supreme Being

Confronted by choices and decisions:
    Each having their own consequences,
    perhaps as described by Sartre
	Awaiting the arrival of the New Kingdom

Part of a drama:
    That is almost incomprehensible
    From which there is "No Exit"
    perhaps as described by Sartre
	Happy with the joys of everlasting peace with God

Requiring tolerance of ambiguity and uncertainty in:
    Predicting the course of our lives
    Accepting genuine risks of chance events
	Confident that we are the intended beneficiaries of eternal blessings

Accepting of the certainty of death	Confident of how life and the afterlife will unfold consistent with our beliefs
Savoring the opportunity to direct ourselves and discover our path to peace and harmony	Comfortable with fate as God decides it

Q & A

You talk about the human condition. Isn't this stuff just for philosophers and philosophy majors?

I find these notions to be both challenging and thought-provoking, too. We will be considering very substantial life issues that have a serious pragmatic history. The issues of life and living are for everyone and especially those who want to discover a better path in life.

Table 5.1, Natural World vs. Supernatural World is pretty heavy duty stuff too. Did you have in mind that we would get all of this done by the final chapter?

We have a good start on sorting out some serious issues of living and dying. There is nothing to memorize or recite. These issues of a natural life in a natural world will emerge more clearly in the chapters that follow.

Chapter 6
Is this Problem Real?
Fear of the Dark and Death Anxiety

Overview

The childhood fear of the dark is a metaphor and model for adult fears of ambiguity, uncertainty and death. We grapple with the scope of the problem of death phobia and examine an exercise for keeping our priorities in order.

Quotations

Man is a marvelous curiosity... he thinks he is the Creator's pet... he even believes the Creator loves him; has a passion for him; sits up nights to admire him; yes and watch over him and keep him out of trouble. He prays to him and thinks He listens. Isn't it a quaint idea? *Mark Twain*

My only fear is that I may live too long. This would be a subject of dread to me. *Thomas Jefferson*

Light be the earth upon you, lightly rest. *Euripides*

Fear of the Dark

As adults, we may look back at the ordinary childhood fear of the dark with some puzzlement. The experience of stark fear and emptiness, the lack of support, the concern that we are left to our own devices in dangerous situations, and the belief our fear is entirely reasonable. The fear of the dark is a useful metaphor of our struggles to master challenges of everyday living and the awkward, lingering fear of our own death. I am referring to the ordinary dictionary definition of death.

As adults we might be dismissive of even the notion that the childhood fear of the dark is in any way comparable to every-day life fears and jitters, much less concern about dying. But for me, the comparison seems to fit. As youngsters, we live in a world of unknowns in which we are assisted by parents and others. We quickly understand we need guidance and coaching to figure out what to do next and to avoid those awkward tearful spells in which everything has gone bad and, on top of that, parents may be upset with us.

Phobia, "an exaggerated usually inexplicable and illogical fear of a particular object, class of objects, or situations, (c.f. http://www.merriam-webster.com/dictionary/phobia) can be very troubling and have a disruptive impact on our functionality. Phobia adversely affects flexibility, mobility, and energy levels. It has received substantial attention in the mental health professions. In more severe cases the problem can be totally disabling and prevent people from living a normal and satisfying life. But, is fear of death a real issue? Is there a real problem here experienced by every-day people in the course of their lives?

Viewed from a contemporary vantage point, the fear of death is like other fears, but dramatically more disabling. Since there is no way to avoid and death issues in daily living. Fear of heights, stage fright and anxiety about flying in commercial airliners are other instances of common phobias. As kids, we may grow up with a variety of fears, including fear of the dark. Parents know about this, because even if they didn't personally experience it, they certainly

Chapter 6 : Is this Problem Real?

know someone who has. The remedy is usually quite straightforward, starting with a low-power light in the child's room. This in turn might be faded down to a small light in the hallway, and further down to an LED plug-in nightlight in the hallway. One principle involved here is adaptation. Early on, the light bulb provides easy visibility and substantial reassurance. The youngster is able to adapt in a series of steps down to a navigational light that allows both children and adults to walk in an otherwise dark room.

Could we ever adapt to the fear of death? It's probably a good idea to deal with our fears of life and living along the way. This is no small matter, since life may have a variety of setbacks and losses by disability or loss of loved ones. However, coping with life is a tall order in itself. If we could begin to cope with the fear of death, taking just a step at a time, not unlike reducing light in the bedroom and hall in stages, we can adapt and become more comfortable. Could we ever look back on the fear of death and think of it in our adult years like the growth and adjustment process of overcoming fear of the dark? Yes, we can.

Consider the challenge of understanding the situation we face. As we age, the end can only be nearer. Adults are every bit as disadvantaged in dealing with the fear of death as youngsters are in dealing with the fear of the dark. We may have grown up with a family or religious tradition that dealt with questions of death in a manner that was not comfortable. For example, the family religion taught one thing and the parents reflecting another. For others, the preparation for dealing with a family death is not sufficient to cope with our experience of the dilemma. It will be good to cut ourselves a little slack here.

Any consideration of the fear of death should be understood against a background of history that powerfully tilts in the opposite direction, namely that death phobia is unlike any other fear. *The Psychology of Death*, (Kastenbaum, 1992, pp.137-138), provides a helpful synopsis of Freudian thinking about death anxiety. Note that in the following quotation Kastenbaum cites an earlier author who was a major advocate of this point of view:

> The fear of death is not to be explained away as a superficial and a disguised representation of a "deeper" conflict. Quite the opposite. Anxiety, all anxiety, is rooted in the awareness of our mortality. The consequences are enormous, and reveal themselves in virtually every aspect of individual and cultural life. The late Ernest Becker (1973) was a leading proponent of this view. . . .
>
> Ordinary life in today's society is marked by heavy repression of death-related anxiety (which is to say, all anxiety), according to Becker and others. This takes a toll on us. This is why we become conformists. We seek the security that is promised by tying into a system that will meet our dependency needs and help us deny our intrinsic vulnerability. Certain events and experiences may disrupt this "let's pretend" arrangement. We are then faced with the challenge of either restoring the tenuous system of mutual (illusionary) support, or confronting death as aware and vulnerable individuals.

For me, the most salient passages of this quotation are:

- Anxiety, all anxiety is rooted in the awareness of our mortality.
- Ordinary life. . . is marked by heavy repression of death-related anxiety.

I think this is really an obsolete picture and want you to know this image belongs to a world of yesteryear. There have been a variety of new understandings of how anxiety and fear operate and how to treat them. We need to recognize these earlier notions are just not applicable anymore. For me, these quotations conjure a vision of the unconscious mind that resembles demonic possession. It is simply not relevant in an era when we have broadly based humanistic, behavioral, interpersonal systems, and experiential models in contemporary psychology.

What would a more modern picture look like? Below is a rank order list of phobias in the US population, based on an National Institute of Mental Health data. Such lists may not have the highest accuracy or reliability and should be taken only as a "ballpark" indication of incidents:

Table 6.1: Top Phobias: Percent of US Population
1. Fear of public speaking – Glossophobia 74 %
2. Fear of death – Necrophobia 68 %
3. Fear of spiders – Arachnophobia 30.5 %
4. Fear of darkness – Achluophobia, Scotophobia or Myctophobia 11 %
5. Fear of heights – Acrophobia 10 %
6. Fear of people or social situations – Sociophobia 7.9 %
7. Fear of flying – Aerophobia 6.5 %
8. Fear of confined spaces – Claustrophobia 2.5 %
9. Fear of open spaces – Agoraphobia 2.2 %
10. Fear of thunder and lightning – Brontophobia 2 %

(cf. Fear-phobia, 2014)

If this ranking is anywhere near accurate, the fear of death is high on the list of concerns for the general public.

But, there is a wide range of views of the incidence, prevalence and severity fears surrounding death. For example, Kastenbaum (1992, p. 149) concludes that we fear death, "Not very much at all," but bases his conclusion on studies using a rating scale for which they were no norms, raising the question of what a high or low score might be. Is there some other evidence that might be considered to clarify this issue?

A book by psychiatrist Irvin Yalom (2008) *Staring at the Sun: Overcoming the Terror of Death,.* offers what he calls ". . . a deeply personal book stemming from my confrontation with death" (p. vii). The presentation relies heavily on case material from Dr. Yalom's chosen clientele, medical patients with terminal illness. Additionally, he describes a variety of personal experiences that can move a person to deal with death issues. Experiences like grief, dreams, life milestones (college reunion) or estate planning are described as powerful mediators of change. In turn, ideas may have a powerful influence on one's thoughts. He looks at the ideas of Epicurius, the ancient Greek philosopher. I have found the final of these arguments to be most interesting but not necessarily helpful:

> Epicurius's third argument holds that our state of non-being after death is the same state we were in before our birth. Despite many philosophical disputes about this ancient argument, I believe that it still retains the power to provide comfort to the dying. . . . (p. 81)

On the following page he comments:

> I have personally found it comforting on many occasions to think that the two states of nonbeing— the time before our birth and the time after our death— are identical and that we have so much fear about the second pool of darkness and so little concern about the first. (p. 82)

Yalom identifies this as the argument of symmetry and provides a citation of the source in his reference section. I did search out the original material but had no luck in tracking down. Hence I provide quotations from Yalom because they are the closest I can come to Epicurius's original words. While I find this argument to be logical and intuitive, it still presents us with, as Yalom points out in the second quotation, a "comforting" idea. Comforting ideas are not a suitable way to understand the realities of the world in which we live.

Chapter 6 : Is this Problem Real?

Overall, the book is a treasure trove of observation and understanding. Yalom describes what he calls "rippling" as, ". . . concentric circles of influence that may affect others for years, even generations." (p. 83) He argues that we, knowingly or unknowingly influence people around us who in turn influence others. In this process we leave a lingering influence of ourselves. He describes connectedness, the power of presence and empathy that keeps us engaged in life, and diminishes the threat of death. Chapter 6 is a brief memoir entitled, "Death Awareness." Chapter 7 offers, advice to therapists, entitled "Addressing Death Anxiety."

We need to figure out what to make of, *Staring at the Sun*. Dr. Yalom comes equipped with a psychoanalytic theoretical orientation. I have already spoken of what I see as some of the unfortunate qualities in that theoretical model. However Dr. Yalom brings a vast experience in treating death anxiety and a profound philosophical perspective on matters of life and death. His perspective must be taken into account. In light of his profound contribution to this area of study, we need to defer to his experience and wisdom and be persuaded that death anxiety is a very serious clinical issue, especially for his preferred clientele, people with a terminal illness. Based on the In NIMH findings cited above and Yalom's copious clinical observations we can conclude that death anxiety surely is a very real problem to be taken quite seriously.

What about "theoretical objections" I have raised, especially for those of us who are on our path to peace and harmony, including me? Perhaps I've been a bit intemperate, especially in this circumstance. In the real world we need to simply set aside any theoretical issues raised by anybody and look at the evidence. The problem of death is substantial and it is an issue that is difficult to cope with for a very substantial number of people, as indicated in the results of the NIMH survey, reported above. From any worldview, death anxiety is a serious matter.

Comfortable?

What about seniors who are financially comfortable? Senior citizens who can afford independent-living facilities with programming and staffing to assure that they are comfortable? Are there people in this group who hold the view they had enjoyed more than their share of life and they were ready to move on? The best I have are some anecdotes based on personal experience.

While visiting my parents when they were staying in an independent living facility, I had many opportunities to chat socially with other residents. I always noticed that my comments and jokes elicited a variety of thoughts and feelings from the other residents. While it's true that no one said anything like, "I'm hoping to find a way out; if I could end it, I would; why am I being tortured like this?" But many said things like many said things like:

> It's too long.
> It's hard to keep going.
> I've had enough.

Riding the elevator and moving about in the building I never saw anyone who was despondent, or ready to hasten their own passing. But, I did find it striking that many casual chats turned to these rather serious issues. These were people who had the means to pay for the services they received at the facility, certainly worth the money but not inexpensive. What can we make of it?

- Life always remains challenging.
- There are no guarantees of happiness.
  While some of the residents may have needed higher levels of interaction and socialization with others, the program was "one size fits all."
- Independent living is often thought of as the "highest quality service" typically available. But it may not be right for everybody.

Chapter 6 : Is this Problem Real?

My father was age 96 when he died and experienced what seems to be inevitable cognitive decline that comes with such senior age. My mom had never been willing to talk about aging or death and it did not seem to be the right time to begin such dialogues. But, she did tell me about friends who had recently died and explained that she was, "Glad for them, because they had waited a long time," or something to that effect. As I now look back at these reports, I can appreciate, in hindsight, there may have been an opportunity to open a broader discussion about her situation, feelings and unmet needs.

For independent living, a setting and location in which at the end of the evening, residents each go to their own apartment and close the door, there may still be these dilemmas of life meaning and the challenges of reaching out to others when we might feel that we need them. Families are somewhere else. Neighbors are behind their own locked doors for the evening. Everybody knows that any reversal of their health condition requiring, "a trip across the street," (the nursing home) may signal the ending of their life is not far off.

What Should I Do?

There is a straightforward approach to the problem that is offered in *Buddhism Without Beliefs* (Batchelor, 1997):

> WHAT AM I here for? Am I living in such a way that I can die without regrets? How much of what I do is compromise? Do I keep postponing what I "really" want to do until conditions are more favorable? Asking such questions interrupts indulgence in the comforts of routine and shatters illusions about a cherished sense of self-importance. It forces me to seek again the impulse that moves me from the depths, and to turn aside from the shallows of habitual patterns. It requires that I examine my attachments to physical health, financial independence, loving friends. For they are easily lost; I cannot ultimately rely on them. Is there anything I can depend upon? It might be that

all I can trust in the end is my integrity to keep asking such questions as: Since death alone is certain and the time of death uncertain, what should I do? And then to act on them. [sic] (pp. 31- 32)

We need to slow down to focus on what Batchelor offers. This can be a useful exercise for our daily life, posing questions for ourselves and then answering them as a means to be mindful of ourselves and our lives:

1. Q: What am I here for?
   A: _____

2. Q: Am I living in such a way that I can die without regrets?
   A: _____

3. Q: How much of what I do is compromise?
   A: _____

4. Q: Do I keep postponing what I "really" want to do until conditions are more favorable?
   A: _____

5. Q: Since death alone is certain and the time of death uncertain, what should I do?
   A: _____

I think these questions are a powerful personal tool for getting at these issues. A regular review of question number five could be a powerful energizer to help us make the most of our lives. This might easily fit into an existing meditation schedule and become an additional part of identifying who we are and where we are going.

Chapter 6 : Is this Problem Real?

Q & A

As you discuss what you call obsolete pictures of the fear of death (Becker, 1973) and if they are out of date, why not just give us a current view of models that actually work?

These authors have been very influential and have left a long legacy of influence on their successors. Their influence continues to be felt and we need to be prepared to deal with these worldviews if our map of the world is to fit the territory it represents.

Theoretical point of view, or worldview, as you have rendered it here, seems to divide people as much as it unites them, particularly in in the study of behavior. What is that all about?

Behavior, personality and the many other dimensions of how people perceive, think, feel, and react to others is not so simple. If we accept the beginnings of scientific psychology in 1879 in Leipzig Germany it might be tempting to say we should be much further along by now. But I don't think human behavior or even the behavior of the four-legged, six legged and eight legged creatures of the world has become any simpler in the intervening time. Worldview is the mechanism that shapes even the observations we make, much less the conclusions we draw. The science of behavior is still a goal for the future.

Chapter 7
Wholeness in Skepticism?
Healthy Doubts

Overview

The Epicurean paradox and Pascal's wager give a sense of the risks of believing propositions offered to us to explain how the world works. We consider sources of bias in and how we communicate with others. We examine a DIY religion that provides a burlesque example of how we might go astray.

Quotations

Faith is believing something you know ain't true. *Mark Twain*

Reality provides us with facts so romantic that imagination itself could add nothing to them. *Jules Verne*

Extraordinary claims require extraordinary evidence. *Carl Sagan*

Skepticism: the mark and even the pose of the educated mind. *John Dewey*

The natural cause of the human mind is certainly from credulity to skepticism. *Thomas Jefferson*

> Blind belief in authority is the greatest enemy of truth.
> *Albert Einstein*

Believe it or Not?

The question of whether or not to believe some proposition offered to us has long been a challenge. Perhaps a way to start is to look at what is known as "the Epicurean paradox" or "the riddle of Epicurus" [341–270 BCE] (Epicurus Riddle: The Problem of Evil, 2012). Note that there are various renditions of this riddle and that what appears below is a common rendition:

> Is God willing to prevent evil, but not able?
> Then he is not omnipotent.
> Is he able, but not willing?
> Then he is malevolent.
> Is he both able and willing?
> Then whence cometh evil?
> Is he neither able nor willing?
> Then why call him God?
> Epicurus

I'm not so sure that the question should be the exact wording of what is now preserved only in secondary sources, but rather that we get hold of a problem in the era of ancient Greek philosophy, before the Christianity emerged. Philosophers classify Epicurus as a skeptical philosopher and that doubt comes through quite clearly in his riddle. This kind of proof of God is known in philosophy as "arguing from evil." What the riddle brings us to is a direct confrontation with two critical themes that logically cannot both be true. Epicurus is inviting us to reject the argument for an external personal God. My point here is simply we are dealing with long standing questions that need to be looked at thoughtfully (cf.: Adams & Adams, 1991).

Chapter 7 : Wholeness in Skepticism?

It seems to me that the problem here is the incongruity and logical inconsistency between the presence of evil and the presence of an all-powerful God. Notice that, from a more modern standpoint, it's wise to look at concepts (like goblin or ghost) and then ask questions about whether there's any verifiable supportive evidence, validity, reality, etc. of the idea. Epicureans leaves us with a logical contradiction that strongly argues against accepting the notion of a personal God. There are many other kinds of arguments and this debate has been underway for a couple of thousand years. I'm not sure it serves us very well to go much further with it. I raise the issue to point up the importance of logical, and critical thinking together with skepticism and problem solving (cf.: Schellenberg, 2007).

Another question of what is reasonable to believe about our world, and the question of the existence of a personal God, is known as Pascal's Wager. The French mathematician Blasé Pascal [1623-1662] put forward an argument that would appeal to agnostics, someone who believes that it is impossible to prove God's existence. His argument, excerpted from Thomas (2012) is as follows:

God either exists or he does not.

If we believe in God and he exists, we will be rewarded with eternal bliss in heaven.

If we believe in God and he does not exist, at worst all we have forgone is a few sinful pleasures.

If we do not believe in God and he does exist we may enjoy a few sinful pleasures, but we may face eternal damnation.

If we do not believe in God and he does not exist, our sins will not be punished.

Would any rational gambler think that the experience of a few sinful pleasures is worth the risk of eternal damnation?

Pascal

Many objections have been raised to the implications of Pascal's Wager. I think it's critical that we not get too deeply bogged down in philosophical or theological arguments, since many of our forbearers have already demonstrated that we are talking about eternal questions. What strikes me is that Pascal has looked only at one side of the question, namely, "What if we don't believe?" Clearly, the other side of the question is, "What if we do believe?" That is, could believing:

Change our behavior?
Make us servants to someone else's agenda?
Intimidate and enslave us to beliefs and practices that are of little merit?

The simple example is, if the surgeon says, "Without this surgery you will die of a brain hemorrhage." I think we have to ask, "Are there any risks the surgery, or the procedures required to deliver the surgery, might possibly be damaging?" That is, given the choice point, "Are there risks to not acting?" But also, "Are there risks to acting?"

To follow-up on the thought of a possible change of behavior, let's look at the very old notion of the "spontaneous generation of flies." I first learned about this old saw in high school biology and was interested to see that there's plenty more than we got hold of when I checked on its history (Spontaneous Generation, 2012). It was originally an Aristotelian notion that flies would spontaneously emerge out of meat and it apparently drew wide acceptance because it fit with the idea of a supernatural creation in which a personal God had produced earth and the heavens. Francesco Redi (1668) found that flies emerged on uncovered meat and when adult files could successfully lay eggs. But, it was a controversial finding. The matter was resolved much later (1859) with a study performed by Louis Pasteur. What we have here is a cherished idea offered by Aristotle of the sort that researchers would later call "armchair speculation." It was only resolved as researchers "got their hands dirty" doing the empirical (laboratory) studies.

Although not the first to do so, Daniel Dennett, *Breaking the Spell: Religion as a Natural Phenomenon* (2007), has urged scientific research on religious themes, topics, and content arguing that religion is a natural phenomenon. While he acknowledges that there are risks to such an undertaking, he argues that it is worthwhile to pursue this line of development. He raises questions about whether there is a biological advantage favoring the dispersion of genes because of belief and how can folk-religions metamorphose into organized religions. This is certainly a controversial book that at least raises a variety of questions about whether we should just believe what we're told by partisans.

Predilection

In *The Religious Mind* (2012) Jonathan Haidt, a social psychologist, points out that there are powerful social influences which regulate our behavior. In radical summary, we speak and act to conform to the social expectations of the people around us. Hence, the hope for independent and critical thinking, at least in a social situation, is not to be taken seriously. If we need objective deliberations, consider the formal debate, the adversarial relationship of plaintiff and defense attorneys in the courtroom or the peer-reviewed scholarly journal. These mechanisms have been institutionalized for many years because of the commonsensical recognition of social influence. What Haidt and others have demonstrated with research evidence is that unless there is some mechanism for critical review of what we say, chances are we are influenced by the social group to whom we speak, of which we are a member, or to which we aspire. Briefly, consider the invited speaker who gives a talk to a clergy group but is not so sure of their religious heritage when he's preparing the talk. Is the preparation likely to be any different if the group is Roman Catholic, Protestant, or Buddhist? How about the speaker who returns to his hometown high school to deliver an address at "homecoming?" Do you think they will have any bad things to say about the local team, about the town, about the conduct of the events that day? Or consider the speaker who is an applicant for membership in the local Kiwanis club? Do you think they will have anything negative to say about the valuable community building activities of the club? Perhaps we need to be asking ourselves whether what we have presumed to be eternal questions, like the meaning of life, what is justice, and whether freedom really matters, may be subject to awkward social influences.

You may be asking yourself whether Haidt and others are to be taken seriously about this, and if so, what it says about getting a fair hearing for ideas. An important question. I think we have to be aware of the dilemma of the search for fact, truth, reality, etc. What emerges is that rather formal structures are necessary to ensure that as a society we have a fair chance at getting community needs met instead of the needs of "information brokers." Consider some examples of institutions that have worked for us historically. The court of law in which an adversarial process brings out opposing positions and the jury decides; the formal political debate in which opposing positions are developed by the debaters and voters decide, or the scholarly journal system in which articles are reviewed by peers in a rigorous and critical fashion with an editor, or editorial board, making final decisions.

Haidt provides a good summary of powerful sources of bias in decision-making. These notions are not new or out of the mainstream of social psychology at all. But, I found it very helpful that in talking about very polarizing ideas he has identified several mechanisms that we can all count on to make polarization worse, not better. In alphabetical order, here is my radical summary of some of his cautionary points:

> **Audience effect-** Influence of the audience on the speaker. Messages are tailored to the audience by being responsive to their sensitivities and hence avoiding anything that would set

them, or put us, in bad standing from their point of view. In effect, we censor ourselves depending on the audience to whom we are speaking.
Confirmation bias- Seeking out and reporting information that supports our point of view of a topic or question.
Demonizing- Assigning to opponents an inferior and evil position in which they are
trying to undermine the truth that we are telling.
False "reasoning"- Using after-the-fact arguments combined with justification to
draw the conclusion with which we started.
Sacralizeing- Assigning the quality of sacredness to our point of view and defending it from other viewpoints at all cost. Once a position is made sacred it is no longer subject to conflicting evidence.

Is there any reason to be skeptical, to apply critical thinking to the variety of thoughts and ideas that compete for our attention in our daily lives? I would think so. Otherwise, we are stuck with accepting the agenda of anybody who asserts a point of view. Does it matter what we believe? The great tyrants of our history immediately come to mind, like Hitler and many others. But what about those who espouse positive and conciliatory ideas and then perpetrate something like The Holy Inquisition implemented by an institutional office created by Pope Paul III in 1542 (Inquisition, 2012)? On one hand, the Roman Church offered reassurance and moral guidance while simultaneously committing atrocities (cf.: *Secret Files of the Inquisition*, 2006).

Are there any risks to adopting, in an uncritical fashion, whatever ideas come to us in the marketplace of thought? Magical thinking is not much of a basis for formulating or analyzing ideas. Perhaps the simplest way to make sense out of the question of whether we might believe anything we are told is by applying the metaphor of the map we are handed and the actual territory that it represents. An ordinary example involves driving instructions to go from St. Paul to Minneapolis. If the instructions tell you to cross the Hudson River on the George Washington Bridge, would we want to get suspicious? Simply put, the map does not fit the territory. We might make ourselves the servants of foolish errands if we don't apply some ordinary common sense.

Do it Yourself?

Brian Gallagher (2012) offers, *How to Create Your Own Religion in Ten Easy Steps*! Gallagher tossed in a bonus step called, "Getting the word out." By my count, he offers 11 "easy steps." In the interest of economy, I have provided an excerpted version from his web page that uses just six of his original eleven steps. Of course he is raucous, outrageous, and fun-poking. However, I think there is a larger point here. Growing up with theological constructions that are elaborate and complicated in the service of the very scary, sub-rosa understanding that we all die, pushes us in the direction of willing suspension of disbelief and we are ready to buy into almost anything:

> **Create a God.** One with a catchy name is best.
>
> **Make it easy for people to "buy into" the worship of your New God.** As you go throughout your daily lives I'm sure you'll find many other ways to acknowledge the divine wonderfulness of The Great God Lardicus through your everyday activities.
>
> **Make it ambiguous.** The Great God Lardicus, a "Dark God" bent on destroying The Temple Of Your Physical Being, or is he a "Light God" and the patron of those who are too busy in their lives to stop and eat a well-balanced meal?
>
> **You need an opposing force.** Not necessarily an arch-enemy, but an opposite perspective so that people can pick sides and fight over things.

Chapter 7 : Wholeness in Skepticism?

You need to confuse everybody. This will make sure that nobody can be really certain WHAT they believe, because it is all so nonsensical to begin with.

The Big Reward. You know everything you always wished you had in this life? After you die, you'll get it! We promise! Hot women. Cute Guys. Flying Cars…

(Excerpted and edited from Gallagher, 2012)

In poking around on these eternal questions over the years, it has come through that, as usual, we are confronted with a very ordinary problem. From the best I can tell, looking at philosophical or theological proofs, none of them work. On the other side of the coin, what about proofs that God does *not* exist? Well there's a logical problem here, namely, it would require the proof of a negative, and that simply isn't possible. Briefly, to satisfy empirical and logical requirements, proving a negative would require searching "everything and everywhere." The classic example is proving that black swans exist. In everyday experience "all swans are white." But that is just casual observation, or anecdotal information. To be convincing an exhaustive search must be carried out. From outer space the earth might look quite small, but from my house, it looks very large. Then there's the whole problem of outer space itself. Simply put, we are talking about an infinite search. And so, the common logical shorthand is, "You can't prove a negative."

Perhaps we need to deal with these eternal questions the way we deal with everyday life, make the best decision we can and move forward with our lives. That is, we need to prove to ourselves, based on our own experience, that any idea that's offered is really workable for us. But, this is not such a new idea:

> Believe nothing, no matter where you read it or who has said it, not even if I have said it, unless it agrees with your own reason and your own common sense. *Buddha*

You're still asking yourself, "What about *wholeness*?" The chapter title raised the question of wholeness in skepticism. I don't argue that with skepticism we find purity, devotedness, piety or saintliness. But, with skepticism, critical thinking and a search for what fits for us, we can become a more whole person. And so, we need to focus on wholeness, completeness, fullness, and you guessed it, peace and harmony. That is, with problem solving, skepticism, critical thinking, and looking carefully at any notion of the world that we are invited to buy into, we can move much more confidently in the direction we know will be useful to us. Of course there are a few more steps along the path to get to our goal state, which will be developed as we move forward.

Q & A

What is the point of going through these proofs of the existence of God? Is this some kind of exercise in character building?

We have looked at one riddle (Epicurus) inviting us to reject the notion of a personal God, and Pascal's Wager, an invitation to accept the notion of a personal God. There are many more (cf. Jones, 2012).

It seems to me the two propositions we looked at may be useful to us because they give a sense of historical perspective, as well as a sense of what passes for a "proof" in Western thinking. Sometimes it is a pretty thin broth. From the best I'm able to determine, none of the proofs of the existence of a personal God actually work, in the same sense that there is no acceptable proof that humanity really exists on a place called earth (cf. Jones, 2012). I find this stuff a bit of a hassle to get through myself, and I suspect many readers will be sympathetic. If you want to look further at the question of proofs of this nature, Emmanuel Kant, *Critique of Pure Reason*, might be a reasonable place (cf. Kant's Philosophy of Religion, 2012, Sec. 3.1). Think about the dilemma of moral philosophers, theologians, and mere mortals like you and me taking

Chapter 7 : Wholeness in Skepticism?

on arguments about matters that are "infinite," so to speak.

I think it best if we depart from this line of investigation and defer to philosophers, theologians and the like, who might have better training than you and me to deal with this stuff. These debates have gone on for more than 2000 years if you just consider Epicurus as a starting place. There are spiritual, personal, and psychological bases for searching out a path to peace and harmony. Let us go forward in the direction in which we are more likely to find pay-dirt.

What kind of psychologist are you? You talk about The Religious Mind (2012) presenting the view that we are heavily influenced by social circumstances. What happened to Sigmund Freud?

Just having access to this book tells us that we both live in a social world. Social interactions produce powerful psychological influences on us and we would not want to forget it for a moment. Freud is a crucial figure in the history of psychology and his influence is likely to be lasting. In my view, he provides a helpful point of departure for more modern thinking.

How about this business of creating your own religion? Isn't this blasphemy?

I see it as a good antidote for what ails us! By reframing the problem, Gallagher (2012) has given us a chance to rethink some commonly held and everyday notions of how to look at the world. Principles like "opposing force" and "confuse everybody" might be just the remedy to take Western religious tradition a little less seriously and our own personal welfare a little more seriously.

Chapter 8
Does "Spiritual but Not Religious" Really Fit?
SBNG

Overview

We discuss changing word usage and its implications. We consider a possible source of the religious experience and provide a comparison of spirituality and religion. Finally we look at a choice of label to use to refer the kind of spirituality we seek.

Quotations

I believe in God, only I spell it Nature. *Frank Lloyd Wright*
Forgive, O Lord, my little jokes on Thee, and I'll forgive Thy great big joke on me. *Robert Frost*

I distrust those people who know so well what God wants them to do because I notice it always coincides with their own desires. *Susan B. Anthony*

Which is it, is man one of God's blunders or is God one of man's? *Friedrich Nietzsche*

Gods are fragile things; they may be killed by a whiff of science or a dose of common sense. *Chapman Cohen*

Extraordinary claims require extraordinary evidence. *Carl Sagan*

Religion consists in a set of things which the average man thinks he believes and wishes he was certain of. *Mark Twain*

Spirituality and Religion

In my junior year of college, Professor Zucker (philosophy & religion) counseled me that I was a religious man. For him, doubt and concern were the essential qualities. There appears to have been a change of usage over the years and the word "spiritual" has increasingly replaced the word "religious" in our common speech. A modern way of clarifying Professor Zucker's point is that I am comfortable with my personal definition of spirituality in which no deity or supernatural or magical power is invoked. My notion of spirituality includes the personal rather than public experience, being part of a cosmic scheme, a search for inner peace and a sense of belonging. What is more, I suspect that I am not very different from anyone else. Many people who may be indignant about my theological views probably share this personal sentiment.

It's not clear that a person with my religious sensitivities and theological exception to most of the institutional religions can really find a place with the recently coined, "spiritual but not religious" (SBNR) group. While there is a change in language and words used, the notion of spiritual, but not religious carries many more meanings than I wish to endorse. Robert Fuller (2001) in, *Spiritual but Not Religious: Understanding Unchurched America* clarifies the current usage of this reference:

> A large number of Americans identify themselves as "spiritual but not religious." It is likely that perhaps one in every five persons could describe themselves in this way. This phrase probably means different things to different people. The confusion stems from the fact that the words "spiritual"

Chapter 8 : Does "Spiritual but Not Religious Really Fit?

and "religious" are really synonyms. Both connote belief in a Higher Power of some kind. Both also imply a desire to connect, or enter into a more intense relationship, with this Higher Power. And, finally, both connote interest in rituals, practices, and daily moral behaviors that foster such a connection or relationship. (p. 5)

My discomfort with the reference to a "Higher Power" centers on , just which Higher Power? It's clear to me that great powers constantly pervade our world. For example, we live in a solar system, which is part of a larger universe with are powerful entities and forces like energy, mass and gravity. The earth brings additional powerful forces, like weather, seasons and the lifecycle of living creatures. While I am convinced of higher powers all around me, they all come down to nature. Consider the notion of a personal God who looks out for our welfare. Note the contradicting example, if we are in conflict, whom does God favor?

Fuller goes on to point out:

Spirituality exists wherever we struggle with the issue of how our lives fit into the greater cosmic scheme of things. This is true even when our questions never give way to specific answers or give rise to specific practices such as prayer or meditation. We also become spiritual when we become moved by values such as beauty, love, or creativity that seem to reveal a meaning or power beyond our visible world. An idea or practice is "spiritual" when it reveals our personal desire to establish a felt-relationship with the deepest meanings or powers governing life. (Fuller Quotes, 2001)

In my high school general science class we had an introduction to the microscope and viewed prepared slides and materials provided by the teacher. I brought in water from one of the local ponds and was able, for the first time, to see amoeba, paramecia and other microscopic creatures that I had been wading around with just a few years earlier. The experience brought a sense of engagement and further stoked my curiosity for learning and understanding. This kind of wonderment, while based on a thirst for knowledge, is also spiritual for me.

I understand that many people have what they describe as religious or spiritual experiences, but where might they come from? There are some ideas that offer interesting glimpses of what may be happening. Durkheim's, *The Elementary Forms of the Religious Life* (1912) offers a powerful explanation of the religious experience as a phenomenon of the social group. He argues that the religious or spiritual experience comes from the fundamental social phenomena of people gathering into a group with common purpose.

> According to Durkheim, a religion is created out of moments of what he calls "collective effervescence." Collective effervescence refers to moments in societal life when the group of individuals that makes up a society comes together in order to perform a religious ritual. During these moments, the group comes together and communicates in the same thought and participates in the same action, which serves to unify a group of individuals . . .
>
> The next step in the creation of religion is the projecting of this collective energy onto an external symbol. As Durkheim argues, society can only become conscious of these forces circulating in the social world by representing them somehow. The power of religion must therefore be objectified, or somehow made visible, and the object onto which this force is projected becomes sacred. This sacred object receives the collective force and is thereby infused with the power of the community. It is in this way that a society gains a tangible idea, or representation, of itself. When

Chapter 8 : Does "Spiritual but Not Religious Really Fit?

> discussing these matters, Durkheim is careful to use the word "sacred object" to describe what is traditionally understood in the West as a God . . . (Emile Durkheim, IEP)

Durkheim is arguing that people misunderstand a powerful social processes and then apply the label "God" to their experience. There are entire knowledge domains studying these issues that get labels like history, philosophy of religion, psychology of religion and sociology of religion. But, is there any intuitive leg-up to help us understand how people might behave so that we can better understand what Durkheim describes?

A helpful psychological study of religion applied criteria to select study participants, who they defined as either religious or spiritual. Religious "dwellers" tend to accept traditional forms of religious authority. They inhabit a space created for them by established religious institutions and relate to the sacred through prayer and public communal worship. By contrast, for spiritual "seekers," individual autonomy takes precedence over external authority and the hold of tradition-centered religious doctrines. Spiritual seekers are explorers who typically create their own space by borrowing elements from various religious and mystical traditions. They frequently blend participation in institutionalized Eastern religion with Western practices. What differentiates dwellers and seekers is not the seriousness of effort to incorporate personal ideals in their lives but their relation to religious authority and tradition (excerpted and adapted from Wink & Dillon, 2003).

Below is a table that is loosely based on the theme offered by Wink & Dillon (2003) providing an example of how these notions work. The table offers a comparison of the polar extremes of spirituality and religion. As in all such comparisons, this is a simplification and there are always exceptions.

The problem here is, concerns about superstition and magic are not resolved, but only sharpened by the above discussion. To recap, we've identified changing use of the words "religious" and "spiritual," and a likely social origin of religious or spiritual experiences as described by Durkheim (Emile Durkheim, IEP). We also looked at the practical application of what are known as operational definitions of religion and spirituality used by Wink & Dillon (2003) to identify the personal styles of their study participants. As Fuller (2001) points out, both of these notions commonly refer to a higher power and connote interest in rituals and practices. As we have discussed, resorting to non-natural forces, like superstition or magic, will not help us, since our major goal is to develop concepts and logic that will allow us to accurately recognize and cope with the realities of our world.

Chapter 8 : Does "Spiritual but Not Religious Really Fit?

Table 8.1 Comparison of Spirituality and Religion

Spirituality	Religion
There is only one. (Alternatively, there are as many types as there are spiritual people at any given time.)	Hundreds of variations
Personal, emergent and individual	Institutional, organized and structured
Chosen experiences	Prescribed practices
Question, reason and accept the consequences	Obedience / Adherence
Novel and personal	Carry on traditions
Emphasis on the present, the here and now	Emphasis on the past and in the future
Expands consciousness	Offers eternal life
Cultivates personal responsibility	Provides order and certainty

Excerpted & adapted from:
http://www.bibliotecapleyades.net/mistic/mistic_10.html
Extension of a theme from Wink and Dillon (2003)

Note that the "regular spirituality," outlined above, provides a clear contrast with religion but it still carries the burden of some unspecified higher power. In my search for an appropriate label to convey only the meaning I wish to express, the most fitting phrase I came up with is "spiritual but no God" (SBNG). This is my attempt to distinguish my world view from "spiritual but not religious" (SBNR), which includes a supernatural power. As we have discussed, the notion of a remote personal God looking after us simply cannot work. We previously talked about what such a God should do if two people are in conflict. Does God play favorites? Then there is our experience of natural disasters and the rest of the events that are adverse to life on earth. For me this is not a difficult decision to make, since I view the world from a naturalistic, freethought vantage point.

Below are two simple lists of the applicable worldly qualities and personal experiences of the concept which distinguish the SBNG spiritual perspective:

List 8.1: SBNG World View

Worldly Attributes:
Natural world
No supernatural powers
No magic
No personal God
No rituals
No invocations

Personal Experiences:
Beauty
Love
Acceptance
Creativity
Wonderment
Participation
Belonging
Solidarity
Life energy
Part of a larger whole
Peace
Harmony

Chapter 8 : Does "Spiritual but Not Religious Really Fit?

Spiritual but not religious (SBNR) does not fit for me because of the excess meanings it carries. Looking at any concept like "God" or "ghost" is a bit more challenging than it may first appear. However, there is help in the form of the principle of parsimony. It tells us that the simplest of various competing explanations is preferable to more elaborate or complicated explanations. While the existence of a word suggests that there may be an underlying reality it provides no evidence that the thing named by the word really exists. For example, concepts like intelligence or personality need to be tested for construct validity and reliability (Is there actually something in the real world that this label relates to and can it be observed repeatedly over time?) before they could be accepted as legitimate.

For now, I can be quite comfortable living in my own little box I call SBNG.

Q & A

OK. It sure comes through that institutional religion is not for you. What is more, you reject a widely held notion of spirituality since, in current usage it refers to a personal God. But do we have to accept this along with all of your other ideas?

It's all up to you. We all need to test out, not only these ideas to see if they can work for us, but all others you come across.

How does it make any sense that you quote Emile Durkheim, a sociologist, when talking about religious experiencing? Doesn't all of this come from God?

That is the question at the heart of the matter. Does the word God really refer to something that has independent existence? Durkheim was a social scientist of very high stature and a major thinker. He was looking for a simpler understanding consistent with principle of parsimony. I find his ideas quite compelling.

If there is no external, personal, super-natural God that looks after us, how is it that these ideas recur across many religions and world views over the centuries?

Here is my guess. The after-life is like a "get out-of jail-free-card," it is like the promises of politicians capaigning for office, it is our "fondest dream come true," it is the happy thought that makes our spirits soar. Jonathan Haidt (2012), a social psychologist, points to what is called confirmation bias. That is, we are especially ready to believe ideas that confirm what we already want to believe. How about we go the other way? Let's use a map that is most likely to fit the territory.

Chapter 9
Something Magical?
Natural Spirit

Overview

We look at the possible origin of spirituality. While it might have seemed to come from a religious quest, there are indications that spirituality is universal and independent of religion.

Quotations

Great works are performed not by strength, but by perseverance. *Samuel Johnson*

It always seems impossible until it's done.   Nelson Mandela
All men should strive to learn before they die what they are running from, and to, and why. *James Thurber*

Meditation is the journey from sound to silence, from movement to stillness, from a limited identity to unlimited space. *Sir Ravi Shankar*

Could Spirituality be Natural?

We have come to that critical place where, at least for me, the preferred choice is spiritual, but no God. While researching this book, I have identified many sources that offer tidbits on this issue but few offer much of substance. There are many highly recommended books that present a serious discussion of atheism, but I find few references to spirituality. My search has not been for spirituality in theism, deism, agnosticism or atheism (See: Mini-Glossary) but rather, for spirituality with peace and harmony. I have found few sources that seriously address these issues.

Spiritual Atheism: The Way of Wisdom, (Sorensen, 2012) offers what he calls, "One man's perspective on life and how to live it." The book is clearly utopian in ambition, and makes an effort at reconciliation in a world of conflicting ideologies. Multiple references to a God that is never defined in the early chapters are quite discouraging. For example, distinguishing between concepts and their actual referent in the world is useful but the question does not seem to get much further. What is offered are some basic definitions useful only to help people confirm that they're actually talking about the same thing. Ultimately the book fails to develop a line of argument supporting the views of the author or a methodology for discovering what to actually do to understand either spirituality or atheism. We will need to look elsewhere for useful insight into the nature of spirituality.

Amy Wallace (2013), *Fear of Death: It's About Life, Actually. Let's Talk About It,* easily escapes the trap of advice giving in favor of offering concepts and explanations, like taking ownership, surrendering and being present. Wallace provides explanations of the understandably confusing issues surrounding our everyday emotional lives and the issues of death. It offers meditations and journaling questions for the reader and an implicit invitation for the reader to track their reactions to the text.

Wallace offers a straightforward explanation of critical issues for living anddying. Why don't we talk about death? Why should we talk about death? Practices for more conscious living and dying. For each chapter she provides journaling questions to prompt readers to look carefully at their own personal situation.

Contemporary French philosopher Andre Comte-Sponville (2007) offers *The Little Book of Atheist* Spirituality. He notes that he

Chapter 9 : Something Magical?

began with no intention to write a large book and the text is limited to just three chapters. Chapter 1 looks at the question, "Can We Do Without Religion?" After looking at who we are and what religions are, and many dimensions of the human experience, he concludes:

> It is possible to do without religion but not without communion, fidelity or love. In these matters, what we share is more important than what separates us. Peace to all, believers and nonbelievers alike. Life is more precious than religion; this is where inquisitors and torturers are wrong. Communion is more precious than churches; this is where sectarians are wrong. Finally--and this is where fine people are right, whether they believe in God or not--love is more precious than hope or despair. (pp. 66-67)

In the second chapter he provides a helpful review of major proofs of God and, like many of us, he found that they didn't work either. Here is how he answers (resolves) to the questions posed in six well-known proofs of God's existence:

The weakness of the opposing arguments, the so called proofs of God's existence.

Common experience: If God existed, he should be easier to see or sense.

My refusal to explain something I cannot understand by something I understand even less.

The enormity of evil.

The mediocrity of mankind.

Last but not least, the fact that God corresponds so perfectly to our wishes that there is every reason to think he was invented to fulfill them, at least in fantasy; this makes religion an illusion in the Freudian sense of the term.

> Taken separately or together, these arguments by no means constitute a proof of God's nonexistence. I said as much at the outset. Does God exist? We do not know. We never shall know- not in this life, at least. Whence the question of whether to believe in him or not.... (p.131)

What Comte-Sponville provides are answers to questions raised in the course of the history of philosophy. He compares and contrasts worldviews, so as to provide us with the current status of some these important questions:

> Not believing in God does not prevent me from having a spirit, nor does it exempt me from having to use it.
> People can do without religion, as I showed in the first chapter, but they cannot do without communion, fidelity and love. Nor can they do without spirituality. Why should they? Being an atheist by no means implies that I should castrate my soul. The human spirit is far too important a matter to be left up to priests, mullahs or spiritualists. It is our noblest pearl, or rather our highest function, the thing that makes us not only different from other animals (for we are animals as well), but greater than and superior to them. "Man is a metaphysical animal," said Schopenhauer and therefore, I would add a spiritual animal as well. This is our way of inhabiting the universe and the absolute, which inhabit us. What could be better, loftier or more fascinating than the spirit? Not believing in God is no reason to amputate a part of our humanity, especially not *that* part! Renouncing religion by no means implies renouncing spiritual life. (pp. 134-135)

Clearly Comte-Sponville (2007) is arguing that spirituality is a fundamental human experience that occurs apart from any attempt to seek out a supernatural being. He is telling us he believes spirituality is natural experience. A major component of his offering is in the form of instances of phenomenological (See Mini-Glossary)

Chapter 9 : Something Magical?

experience described by important figures. He is gentle and respectful of the reader's sensitivity but never wavers in positing his own views. Under headings like the following he reminds us of experiences we have all had:

> Mysticism and Mystery
> Immensity
> The Oceanic Feeling
> A mystical experience
> Is It Possible to Speak about Silence?
> Mystery and Self Evidence

Again, these topics are not offered as proofs and the Comte-Sponville presents them only for our consideration, not with any identifiable dogmatic intent. As indicated by some of the sub-chapter headings, as above, Comte-Sponville provides an engaging style to bring his notion of spirituality to an intellectual dimension so that we might understand it:

> Whether or not you believe in God, the supernatural or the sacred, you are confronted with the infinite, the eternal and the absolute--and with yourself. Nature suffices. The truth suffices. Our own transitory finiteness suffices. Otherwise we could not conceive ourselves as being relative, the ephemeral or finite. (p.136)

Comte-Sponville shows us how we may recall our own experience of these phenomena rather than attempting to tell us about them. But you ask, why go to an atheist for a notion of spirituality? My logic is straightforward. An atheist, especially a scholar (philosopher) from the atheist camp has no ax to grind. In this case, Comte-Sponville has nothing to gain or lose with his analysis of spirituality. It can't make his theological position look more attractive and it can't put him into a position of higher influence with the atheists, since his line of argument is generally not favored in the data and fact driven atheist camp. For me, Comte-Sponville (2007) is in a position to be an honest broker and has nothing to gain from being anything else.

Now, consider the position of this writer. What might I have to gain in this argument about God versus no God or spirituality versus religious experience? Perhaps there might be some advantage for me in one direction or another, but I can't think of any advantage in either direction. I believe that I am also in a position to be an honest broker, but I will defer to your judgment (the reader) in the long run.

I think there is potential for misunderstanding in quoting the words of a self-declared atheist Comte-Sponville (2007). Notice the (now archaic) usage of the word Christian as a way of saying, good, kindly, or charitable. Consider, "That was really Christian of you." Can we possibly imagine a similar usage of the word "atheist"? For example, "That was really atheist of you (meaning kind). In contrast, what are the connotations of the word "atheist?" Polls show, atheists are in an extreme minority in the US it's hard to imagine any such usage. I personally take it as axiomatic that people are not good or bad because of their worldview or theological view. It is their actions, what they do in the world, that matters (c.f. Jefferson quotes). Was Adolf Hitler a regular in his church attendance, whatever his faith? His religious views and church attendance are apart from the question of whether he caused the deaths of millions of people. He fits in the "monster" category, but it has nothing to do with his creed or church attendance. Freethinkers, agnostics and atheists are good people who bring a worldview that's different from religious views, almost anywhere in the world.

One of the pieces that comes through here is that, even though we've been told on good authority that, in our era, many people use the words religious and spiritual synonymously (Fuller, 2001) Comte-Sponville (2007) and this writer choose to define and use them quite differently. While almost certainly in the minority, we use the word spirituality to refer to an internal or phenomenological

Chapter 9 : Something Magical?

experience referenced by many writers and very different from religious practice. I think it is quite clear that it is worth making a distinction between them.

Hemlock?

Looking at the issues of worldview we must consider the possibility that even though some philosophies or religions are time honored, there are newer ideas that better encompass the problems and decisions we face in our world. If we look at some alternative ways of considering the world around us and those particular ways turn out to be unpopular or even insulting to people of a particular point of view, should we be punished by our friends and neighbors? This was certainly the case in the experience of a famous philosopher:

> In 399 BC, Greek philosopher Socrates was sentenced to death for the corruption of Athenian youth. It would come at his own hands as he put an elixir of poison hemlock to his lips and sipped. His pupil, Plato, was present at his death and recalled the events following the fatal dose of hemlock. Socrates walked about the room until his legs and feet grew heavy. As the poison worked its way through his body, numbness ensued and progressed upward until his heart stopped beating and Socrates was dead. (c.f. Socrates-and-his-hemlock, 2014)

Let's just agree in advance, no matter who disapproves of the worldviews we discuss here, nobody drinks Hemlock.

Q & A

How could it be that spirituality is natural? Doesn't it come directly from God?
When using words that have changing usage it's really important to identify the intended meaning. I have tried to do that here as have others before me. About spirituality coming from God, it may be just

the opposite. Perhaps the experience of spirituality raises within us ideas about a protective God.

What if we are still uncomfortable with this natural world identified here?
I think it's fair to say the world we live in has been running millions upon millions of years. With the exception of climate change, it seems to me that the natural world has been doing pretty well for itself very much the way we see it in our lifetimes. During all of natural history, whatever it is that makes the world go seems to have been working OK. I think we can rely on it to continue for millions of years more.

Chapter 10
Could We Skip the Smoke and Mirrors?
Realistic Perspective

Overview

We sample multiple points of view often taken as free-standing and adequate ways to comprehend the world. Just like the golf pro who carefully sights the green from different angles before making the final shot, we want to look at the world from many angles. The several models offered should each contribute in their own way to our perspective on the world we see.

Quotations

Magic is the only honest profession. A magician promises to deceive you and he does. *Karl Germain*

A great deal of intelligence can be invested in ignorance when the need for illusion is deep. *Saul Bellow*

A lie that is half-truth is the darkest of all lies. *Alfred Tennyson*

I know of no society in human history that ever suffered because its people became too desirous of evidence in support of their core beliefs. *Sam Harris*

About the Sandwich Islands, "How sad it is to think of the multitudes who have gone to their graves in this beautiful island and never knew there was a Hell." *Mark Twain*

All I Could See from Where I Stood

One of the fundamental questions in much of this book concerns the problem of how to view the world. An adequate view of the world allows us to comprehend the natural world as we find it. Such a view would need to be functional and realistic, in order to guide us through the realities of the world. As youngsters we have instruction, guidance, and modeling from parents and elders who can point the way. As we move forward in our lives, we need to frame our own system for looking at the world realistically. The understanding we develop can work when we try to get our needs met but also facilitate the development of practical, artistic, scholarly, and scientific understandings. The clear benefit is that we are much more likely to work for us than, starting from a fanciful, romantic or magical way of looking at the events of our world.

We look at the world through the unique prism of our own experience. Life experiences contribute to how we view the world; among them are family legacy, religious heritage, political affiliation, social class, life aspirations, life opportunities and occupation. Not only are we shaped by our life experience, but over time we emerge from our family of origin into adulthood and probably into our own nuclear family. This makes it important for us to transition into new roles and perspectives. In making these changes we need to adjust many of the components that make up the worldview from which we see, experience, and act.

Menu, Sir / Madam?

What I'm proposing is more like a menu of choices rather than a prescription of what you should do. This is a sensitive issue and I feel some urgency to say something about it right up front. Think of our menu as a kind of restaurant menu from which you may

Chapter 10 : Could We Skip the Smoke and Mirrors?

select "one from "Column A," one from "Column B," etc. With the understanding that we live in an interconnected natural and social world, let's take a look at some menu choices from which we might select in formulating an outlook, worldview or perspective with which to look at the natural and social worlds. These groups, organizations or thought traditions, are roughly organized in terms of popular awareness, based only on my guess of how widely known they are in the US and the Western world. Of course, popularity is no indicator of usefulness, much less accuracy, of how the world works. These are options from which you are offered the opportunity to select.

In developing our menu we might start with a **common sense** component, since it has a lot to recommend it as a starting place. This is a choice that probably does not present a lot of conflict for us. This is a practical view of the world which is shared with others around us and they serve as a convenient reference to guide our behavior. There is not much need for instructions to follow or books to read because common sense is widely shared in our social world. The benefits of common sense are that it is easily acquired in the process of childhood and maturing, it is rather close to world of daily experience and becomes quite intuitive as we move forward. A basic fund of knowledge, and an understanding of how our actions impact on the world around us, seems like a critical first step. No one should leave home without it. There do not seem to be good arguments against adopting a common sense component for our worldview so I will place it in "Column A" on our menu.

Naturalism (philosophic) needs to be in our menu. I have certainly argued for a naturalistic point of view in maintaining that we live in a natural world and that magic does not work. I have argued that belief in magic or the supernatural is essentially a reliance on arcane powers. Watching magic shows might be fun, but magic itself doesn't work well for removing snow from the driveway or getting the car repaired. In researching this topic I came upon a website by

John R. Shook which provides a compelling explanation of what naturalism is about. Here is just one paragraph:

> Naturalism emphasizes the progressive and expanding knowledge that observation and science provides. Science continually revises its understanding of physical reality. Today's scientists have new conceptions of energy and matter that most 19th century scientists would have found incomprehensible, and the next century's scientists will likely demand major revisions to today's best theorizing about what physical reality is like. Because science's best ideas about reality undergo improvement, naturalism is a philosophy that requires intellectual humility: while reality is physical and discoverable by science, naturalism cannot offer any final and perfect picture of exactly what this reality is like. Therefore, the primary task of philosophical naturalism is *not* to defend science's current best theories about reality -- science itself is responsible for reasonably justifying its own theories.
>
> **Philosophical naturalism undertakes the responsibility for elaborating a comprehensive and coherent worldview based on experience, reason, and science, and for defending science's exclusive right to explore and theorize about all of reality, without any interference from tradition, superstition, mysticism, religious dogmatism, or priestly authority.** (Bold face in original; Shook, 2006) It's your choice, check under "Column A."

Rationalism is another "reasonable" choice. Thinking, based on examination of reasoned alternatives, with choices based on compelling logic doesn't seem to me like a hard sell. Mathematics, and especially the plane geometry we learned in high school, are examples of very practical applications of a rational approach. Some find plane geometry to be logical and intuitive and others complain, there is nothing we can memorize to make it work since there aren't

Chapter 10 : Could We Skip the Smoke and Mirrors?

strict rules to apply, it is very difficult. As in the above examples, it's hard to argue for irrational thinking or poorly choosing alternatives and so this might still be an easy choice also going into "Column A." A reasonable and logical approach to understanding our world, and making sure to check on how our proposed solutions might backfire, may be pretty hard to argue against.

I would think our *carte du jour* must certainly include a **scientific** alternative, although perhaps it should appear in "Column B. "Why Column B? Because scientific method involves a dramatically higher level of abstraction with formal systematization of how knowledge is generated. As we develop these conceptual frameworks, some will go in their own column based on this kind of reasoning. Along with high school math, there were required science courses. While the whole notion of science may seem a little off-putting at first, any casual review will reveal a very compelling value to scientific discoveries. Germ theory is the easiest for me to recall because of the deadly serious issues with the progress of medicine before this notion arrived on the scene. People died without knowing the potential for infection from deadly pathogens, and without the recognition that they had been infected by microorganisms. Lister, Pasteur, and many others gave us germicides leading to, not just common products like mouthwash, but also safe milk and a less germ infested environment (cf. Germ Theory, 2012).

A simple and helpful frame for understanding the critical features of science is rendered something like this: eliminate or control for any known sources of error in the design and measurement. That is, if you can remove error from your study you might very well have scientifically credible results. Because of the powerful success of scientific ventures, the benefits of this approach are readily seen. While empirical research requires highly trained personnel, substantial facility resources, as well as substantial costs for equipment and materials, the payoff has been very powerful.

Humanism also deserves a place in our *carte du jour*. Perhaps the easiest contrast with humanism is theism and deism. Both incorporate an external supernatural God. The various places I searched for a brief but comprehensive definition seem to have as much trouble as I did rendering the idea. The reference cited below has this and many others from which to choose:

> Believing that it is possible to live confidently without metaphysical or religious certainty and that all opinions are open to revision and correction. [Humanists] see human flourishing as dependent on open communication, discussion, criticism and unforced consensus. (cf. Humanism, 2012)

Humanism occupies a prominent place in Western and American thought. In the US, it is well represented by the American Humanist Association (AHA). Their website has a variety of helpful resources. I think we had better put them under "Column C." A quick inspection of their aspirations indicates they offer six broad reaching principles, the first two of which refer to how we know what we say we know (epistemology) and a naturalistic worldview.

In "Column D" I will put the Unitarian Universalist Association which is the US parent group of churches, fellowships and societies. For the sake of simplicity, I will just refer to them as **UU Churches**. They describe themselves as a liberal religious group with no creedal test. They see themselves as sharing in a search for personal truth. This is a broadly based non-Christian, "big tent" group that meets on Sunday mornings. But I think their words better render their worldview:

> Unitarian Universalism *has no set beliefs*, and that is its defining characteristic. According to a UUA pamphlet:
> With its historical roots in the Jewish and Christian traditions, Unitarian Universalism is a liberal religion -- that is, a religion that keeps an open mind to the religious questions

people have struggled with in all times and places.

We believe that personal experience, conscience and reason should be the final authorities in religion, and that in the end religious authority lies not in a book or person or institution, but in ourselves. (cf.: Unitarian Universalism, 2012)

The benefit of the UU Church perspective is that it does not require any presumptions about the existence of a personal and supernatural God and yet it brings a humane and broadly accepting view of all spiritual traditions. Some UU Churches offer a program of readings and discussions called, "Building Your Own Theology," using a source-book by the same title (Gilbert, 2005) to help individuals develop a sense of what fits for them.

I suspect you're wondering what happened to the rest of the wide range of Christian traditions. As you might guess from the earlier chapters, the Judeo-Christian tradition does not fit very well for me, and hence it's hard to recommend to others. Based on substantial coaching I've prepared a simple typewriter graphic that appears below. The concept came to me from a dear friend, Fred Berkobin, who shared many insights in discussions that I will long remember (1966 f). If you look at a theological spectrum or continuum with the liberals on the left and the conservatives on the right, the various groups might arrange themselves something like this:

Typewriter Graphic 10.1: Christian Theological Spectrum
Liberal   **Conservative**

< -- >
N to ∞   1   2   **∞**

1	Unitarian-Universalist
2	Society of Friends, AKA, Quaker
∞	Liberal Christian, Conservative Christian, Roman Catholic,

Orthodox, etc.

UU Churches and Quakers are at one end of the spectrum and nearly everyone else is at the other.

But maybe it's time to get a bit more specific in looking at where the UU Churches fit on a theological spectrum. Although they come from a Christian tradition, they no longer regard themselves as Christian, nor do they fit the typical tests offered for Christian belief. The point of this minimalist graphic is not to put something onto the UU Churches, or put anything over on you, but to try to demonstrate that they are very far away from even the liberal Christian groups, much less conservative Christian groups, in their thinking.

Buddhism I will place in "Column E." This is one of the thoughtful meditative traditions of the world. Within it are a variety of sects with their own distinctive traditions and approaches to coping with life's problems. I find the teachings of the Buddha (the enlightened one, not a deity) to be logical, intuitive and understandable. I also find myself very attracted to the Buddhist notion of meditative practice, perhaps because it fits naturally and spontaneously into my own historical practice. This kind of distilled, streamlined version of Buddhism is sometimes referred to as, Buddhism without beliefs, presumably after the book by the same name (Batchelor, 1997). For all of us beginners, including me, it might be better to start with a convenient primer that can help with basic understanding of the concepts and practices (cf.: Basics of Buddhism, 2012; Landaw and Bodian, 2003). The benefits of the Buddhist point of view include reasonableness, the lack of a need for an external personal deity, and a broad acceptance of other spiritual traditions. They incorporate commonsensical, rational, naturalistic, humanistic, and compassionate world views. But, I don't ask that you take Buddha's ideas uncritically, and neither would he:

Chapter 10 : Could We Skip the Smoke and Mirrors?

> Believe nothing, no matter where you read it or who has said it, not even if I have said it, unless it agrees with your own reason and your own common sense. *The Buddha*

In our look at Buddhism we want to consider two additions or adjustments to the tradition. First, the substantial emphasis on living in the present with keen personal awareness could distract us from recognizing that we also need to examine, reconsider and turn-over ideas before we accept them or go forward with them. Nothing in the emphasis on mindfulness should prevent us from giving all ideas full scrutiny, even if it might require attention to issues other than the sensations of the moment. This as an opportunity to prevent ourselves from being distracted by second thoughts and misgivings later, when some poorly understood idea backfires.

Second, we need to be able to plan for our future. While this effort will require a focus on a variety of issues that take us out of the moment, in the long run it will save potential missteps and hence make it possible to enjoy more living in our future.

Caution is in order about the many introductions and summaries of Buddhism and also the reactions, characterizations, and warnings by competing religious groups. The primers on Buddhism might be burlesqued as, "three of these, four of these, and eight of these." They might prepare us for an awkward recitation of what might be appropriate for a child to memorize as their "knowledge of Buddhism." I think it's a good idea not to be put off by these simplistic and staccato renditions of a major, competitive tradition of world class thought.

Similarly, while I don't think there's any malicious intent, commentary, summaries, explanations, charts, etc. offered by various Christian traditions, seem to contain misleading and confusing representations of the Buddhist worldview. It might be helpful to watch for what the Buddhist tradition offers as a "description" of the world of human experience which has been misunderstood as a "prescription" of what the world should be. The Buddhist identification of suffering and struggle as primary human problems seems to be misunderstood. Instead, these painful conditions are taken as a statement of what ought to be and the Buddhist worldview is then rejected as a grim and desolate understanding of human life and human nature. Here is an analogy. I had an experience telling a new acquaintance on Ham Radio about a power hook-up using the cigarette lighter outlet in my a newly acquired car. Since I didn't have a chance to run the power cable directly to the battery, I had few alternatives. When my new friend heard that I could only run on low power because of my temporary arrangements, he seemed to think that I was recommending the stop-gap measures I had taken. Just to clarify, I was "complaining" not "bragging." In the case of the Buddhists, I believe they are telling us how they see the human experience rather than how they think it ought to be.

Existentialism is the final menu entry and I will put in "Column F." Again, it needs to stand on its own and not cast a shadow on other parts of the bill-of-fare. Earlier we discussed and enjoyed the benefit of the long quotation from Sartre. The basic argument is that there are problems and challenges associated with life and existence and the natural world prevents us from avoiding the choices in our lives. "The individual creates his / herself by making self-directed 'Choices,' and 'as human existence is self-conscious without being pre-defined, we, as autonomous beings, are 'condemned to be free...'" (Jones, 2012). "Dinner" could not be complete without the existentialist course, at least from my point of view. Sartre is talking about how the natural world works and the necessary relationship between decision and consequence that life brings to us. The existentialist point of view serves as yet another helpful reminder of the need for human action and responsibility.

Clearly these individual world views are not mutually exclusive. That is, they overlap one another to a substantial degree. All of the views are based on common sense, rationality and they have an internal logic. The UU Church view incorporates all of the above and implicitly the existentialists share the notion of individual

Chapter 10 : Could We Skip the Smoke and Mirrors?

responsibility. Perhaps you wonder why include so many individual components. I think it is important to look at the question of emphasis. Scientists of any discipline have a particular focus like physics, chemistry, biology, etc. We are likely to do our best if we appreciate these special emphases of each view to better inform our perspective on the world.

I don't mean to say that this is an exhaustive list of everything that's needed to formulate a worldview, only that with these components we have a reasonable chance of getting a sufficiently accurate view of the world, so we will not be sailing into danger every time we try to take what appear to be prudent actions. Perhaps our dinner menu is better presented merely as an "appetizer" menu, as a kind of prelude to the rest of our lives. In any case, these components of a worldview will help us to better understand what comes up on our horizon and perhaps give us a bit of a bootstrap into figuring out how to cope with the challenges that the natural world provides for us.

Good hunting and *bon appétit*.

Q & A

What do I need all of this for? Isn't common sense plenty?

I don't think so. The example that comes easily to mind is the story about the fisherman troubled about starfish depleting their catch. Their commonsensical solution was to cut the starfish in half and throw them back to let them die. Ironically their problem only got worse. Eventually they got desperate enough to start asking questions of marine biologists. It turns out that biologists understood that starfish have the ability to regenerate limbs hence cutting them in half or cutting off pieces, the fisherman's strategy, was not a very good solution, since it helps to increase the starfish population. (cf.: Starfish... Regeneration, 2012)

Good! So you lay out all this stuff for us. What's your favorite? What's the minimum package that we can make work?

While you are certainly invited to pick and choose, I would encourage you to savor and the entire menu. I finally concluded we are talking about appetizers rather than dinner. It's hard for me to see how anyone can realistically get by with any less than the all these tasty morsels. You will still need a hearty dinner to sustain you.

Chapter 11
True Grit: Magic Too?
Pluck & Rigor

Overview

We examine the meaning of grit and take an additional look at magic. Where does grit come from and how do we get it? Can magic, sleight-of-hand or craving be workable ways of knowing, or provide any help finding our path?

Quotations

Energy and persistence conquer all things. *Benjamin Franklin*
The man who moves a mountain begins by carrying away small stones. *Confucius*

A wise man will make more opportunities than he finds. *Francis Bacon*
It does not matter how slowly you go as long as you do not stop. *Confucius*

Religion consists in a set of things which the average man thinks he believes and wishes he was certain of. *Mark Twain*

Mustering Grit

By grit I mean discipline, persistence, determination, resolve or doggedness. It is one of the major themes of this book, namely perseverance. But this raises the question of just how we could get grit? It would hardly seem to be anything we could eat, drink, or invoke. Notions like grit, personality, cheerfulness, friendliness, seriousness, etc., are descriptors we apply to people after we observe their behavior. So, it is clear that grit isn't anything we could "get," but it surely is something we could exhibit in preparing ourselves for our path.

Consistent with earlier discussion, the last thing we want to do in order to demonstrate grit is to use any kind of brute force. More like it is relax, conserve energy and consider alternatives. The clear implication of grit is prevailing against adversity. For the sake of discussion, I will frame the matter in terms of dealing with an opponent. But, I don't mean to say that we should have adversarial relationships with the people in our lives. Cooperative relationships really do pay off, but good skills are needed to make relationships flourish (Jensen, 1975).

Having briefly played at Judo as a young man, here are some metaphors it offers. As your opponent moves:

> Be as a leaf on the water. Go where the wind takes you.
> Keep the preferred distance, allowing you to deflect verbal or physical strikes.

> If the energy is flowing in the right direction, keep it going.

> Keep your balance, make sure your opponent does not keep theirs.

> Step aside and let your opponent pass by without resistance.

> Position yourself for your next move as they pass through.

> Keep your momentum going.

> Trip-up your opponent when they are off balance.
> Follow through with actions that work for you.

Chapter 11 : True Grit: Magic Too?

We'll need to apply a variety of skills in order to manage our situation as we move toward our path. Here are some basic behavior management principles:

In social situations, attention shapes behavior, ours and that of others.

Manage energy flows (expenditures) carefully:

> Thought
>
> Behavior
>
> Emotion

Stress produces fatigue and a need for rest and recovery. Get needed "R&R."

Focusing on provocative or upsetting events is not helpful and should be avoided.

Relax and let the spooky stuff wash out of your head.

Move forward on stepping stones like crossing a creek by walking on the rocks.

Follow your nose. Do what works.

What we don't say, or do, matters as much as what we actually say or do.

In the table below there are some ordinary Do's and Don'ts that can be useful to guide your behavior.

So where does grit come from? It comes from "all of the above." Grit emerges out of managing ourselves, optimizing who we are, dealing with others in good faith and addressing life problems in direct and timely ways. As we manage, grow and optimize our selves we will find grit and we will be able to move forward on our path.

We will be able to see and feel it in ourselves and it will be subtly observable to others.

Table 11.1 Mustering Grit: Dos and Don'ts

Do	Don't
Conserve energy and resources	Overreact Use yourself down to the nub
Accept feeling statements from others	Take offense
Stick to your goals	Get caught in the agenda of others
Offer an alternative frame of reference	Contest over small points
Put yourself in the place of the other	Insist that others adopt your view
Accentuate the positive	Focus on provocative or upsetting events
Identify your positive personal qualities	Punish yourself with derisive words like dummy, stupid, silly, etc.
Practice exacting personal discipline	Figure it will all work out

Still No Magic

What we are looking for is rigorous thinking that will help us to understand the world more easily and clearly. We need to have an

Chapter 11 : True Grit: Magic Too?

accurate representation of the world, to construct our picture of it in a systematic fashion. We would want to insure not only accuracy but also predictability.

There is a marvelous cartoon by Sidney Harris (sciencecartoonsplus.com) that gets at the issue of magic as a solution to critical problems. Two dignified gentleman are working at a whiteboard with what appears to be a scientific formulation in three steps. One of them is pointing to the middle step which says, "Then a miracle occurs," and explains, "I think you should be more explicit here in step two." The meaning is quite clear. If a scientific, theological, religious, or any other formulation which offers the notion of how the world works, relies on magic it is likely to be more humorous than helpful.

Can we meet our personal needs by wishing, willing or praying? Is there really a fountain of youth? Here is a little ditty that goes back to 1605, in various forms:

> If wishes were horses
> Beggars would ride
> If turnips were watches
> I would wear one by my side.
> (If wishes were horses..., 2012)

These cravings for rain and good crops, eternal life and horses go back to the first rain dance, to the dawn of human kind. It is, of course, a reliance on external and supernatural forces, the practice of magic.

Stuart Vyse in his book, *Believing in Magic: The Psychology of Superstition* (2013), offers a profile of people who do believe in magic. His characterization and is certainly not very flattering but I don't think it's mean-spirited:

> First, without exception, the features of this personality are not very desirable. Our believer is less

intelligent, more conservative, more fearful of death, more susceptible to hypnosis, and more alienated than his or her non-superstitious peers. Some of these characteristics are consistent with the common stereotype of a dull, anxious, and gullible believer in lucky charms and talismans, but there are a few surprises. The stereotype gives us no hint that the superstitious individual should be conservative. Given that the New Age movement has a distinctly antiestablishment flavor, we might reasonably predict the opposite result.

Vyse goes on to offer the caveat that there are individual differences that that such a general statement cannot be applicable in all cases. I do not believe that Vyse is interested in name-calling or derisive labeling and neither am I, but I think what he is pointing to could be helpful to our understanding. We have looked at the issue of worldview as a component of finding our path (chapter 10). In general, the more integrated and broadly based our worldview, the better we will do at understanding the world we live in. By integrated I mean that the pieces need to fit together well and of course broad-based requires and inclusiveness of multiple ways of understanding what we're looking at.

Could any kind of magic or ritual work in any way? The only way such devices can work is as a palliative or a "self-soother" for us. They are a kind of placebo that influences only how we feel but not how the world works. Having confronted a situation that is out of our control, we still take action. After we complete the intervention we can feel better that we have "addressed" the problem, however useless our action might be. I would think it might be more likely if we would try to quiet ourselves, settle, focus on our thoughts, feelings and fears. As we get ourselves into focus, it will be important to take a second look at the problem. Consider the scientists in the cartoon described above.

Chapter 11 : True Grit: Magic Too?

What Could Keep Us from Our Path?

We live in large systems that have their own ways of running. During the past few decades it has been easier to talk about weather systems without too much apology and ecosystems are more widely understood today. A system has multiple interacting parts; change of any part changes all other parts. Slowing or stopping traffic in one part of a metro area will affect adjacent roads. In addition to living in a large social system, we live in family, school, work, community and regional groups that have social and cultural expectations. A helpful exposition and example of multiple interacting systems is provided in the program, *Earth from Space* (2013). It provides analysis and visualization of the relationship between the sun, Earth, seasons, elements, geographic features, wind and sea currents and much more. This is a two hour special program that, "…reveals a spectacular new space-based vision of our planet. Produced in extensive consultation with NASA scientists, NOVA takes data from earth-observing satellites."

There are also family heritage and cultural traditions which powerfully influence us. If you grew up with Hanukah or Christmas celebrations, but fail to follow them, how does it feel? Over the years I have felt the same frustrations dealing with the fireworks on Independence Day in the US. When I attended, I felt disappointed. When I didn't attend, I felt disappointed. Making changes from our early life trajectory can be quite challenging.

If we make a radical change from our "normal," we might be noticed. Questions might follow and, after that, lecturing about how we ought to behave. We put ourselves in line for social pressure and disapproval. Social pressure might be more powerful than expected at first. To paraphrase Jonathan Haidt (2012), the social psychologist discussed earlier, we say and do what we are expected to say and do.

Similarly, peer groups are powerful transmitters of social norms. It might be easy to dismiss peer pressure as high school or college phenomena, but it lasts and lasts. I had the pleasure of talking to a business man from the New York area when I was quite young.

Naively I asked why a guy could not just have lunch at his desk, or in the break room. He described the disapproving stares from peers and social ostracism that followed. There is a now classic book by William F. Whyte, *The Organization Man* (1956), which dramatically develops the topic of organizational conformity. Powerful norms and social expectations regulate our behavior long past our school days.

In short, there are many pressures that militate against personal change and finding our path. We might even get anxious, try to deny, pretend or minimize to help ourselves feel better. What if we find ourselves in a real crunch while searching for our path? Will it help to use-down all of our intellectual and emotional resources to reach our goal; to burn ourselves out to find our path? We know we will need to manage, grow and optimize ourselves in order to go forward. Starting now let's enjoy the process, care for ourselves and make the most of our situation. It will take grit to do this thing, but you already knew that. Now you know that grit is not a thing to get, but rather a process by which we can reach to our goal.

Q & A

I can still do this if I want to, can't I?
Sure you can. I just mean to say again there are a few things that go with the program. Behavior, belief and life change are not simple matters. It takes grit.

Seeking my own path to peace and harmony could just be my own secret. Who will have to know?
People will know only if you tell them. You are in control here. You can say all you want to, or nothing at all.

Will seeking my own path be worthwhile in the long run?
If your current path is satisfactory, why change? If you are looking for something different, perhaps peace and harmony is in the right direction. Do the existentialists say something about making our own choices, creating our destiny? (Sartre, quoted in Jones, 2012)

Chapter 12
Any Relief from the Stress?
Relaxation

Overview

We explore the general notion of relaxation training and focus on a direct, simple, and easy to apply method of inducing relaxation, which I call "breath control relaxation."

Quotations

Be quiet, so that life may speak. *Leo Babouta*

Be still and know who you are. *Kirtana*

Stillness reveals the secrets of eternity. *Lao Tzu*

To be still means to empty yourself from the incessant flow of thoughts and create a state of consciousness that is open and receptive. *John Daido Loori*

In the midst of movement and chaos, keep stillness inside of you. *Deepak Chopra*

Where to Start

Pick your favorite relaxation procedure. It seems like there must be a million of them. Fun distractions like a ballgame, meeting people over coffee, a walk around the block, light exercise in or a hot shower are frequently recommended. The next steps might be soaking in a hot bathtub or in this era of high fashion accessories soaking in the "hot tub" might come in as a top choice. I'm reminded of college and reading about Odysseus stepping from the bath and looking like an immortal God. I frankly didn't make much sense to me at the time and I had trouble figuring out why the professor focused on it. In retrospect I now take it as a tribute to the relaxing power of the bath (Crosthwaite, 2013). I don't think there are any bad choices here but it's worth noticing that the level of mind and peripheral muscle relaxation are important pieces of this puzzle.

Relaxation and meditation are major components of the model for finding a path to peace and harmony. Instructions for deep muscle relaxation are developed below. Meditation is considered in later chapters.

Relaxation training or at least the systematic induction of the deep muscle relaxation response, developed some years ago remains a powerful and effective treatment. It improves just about everything bad except ingrown toenails. A comfortable, self-contained and relaxed state helps to facilitate task completion while having an enjoyable time. It is used as a free-standing procedure to help people settle and feel better and also in conjunction with treatment for intense fear or full phobic reactions (e.g.: desensitization of phobia). These procedures were developed beginning in the 1950's and later, coming out of behavioral models of intervention developed by Joseph Wolpe (1958), Arnold Lazarus (1976), and many others. Do you know anybody who is afraid of heights, flying on airlines, snakes, their boss, high places, small spaces, etc.? These problems are eminently treatable with systematic sensitization or related procedures. Various meditative traditions have understood the relaxing and mind cleansing effects of deep relaxation and contemplation for millennia. How could we know anything much about the outcome of meditation? Easy to ask, but harder to do. What is required are controlled studies of human subjects

Chapter 12 : Any Relief from the Stress?

incorporating careful design, data collection, analysis, interpretation, etc. There are research studies that start to give a few answers (cf. Cahn & Polich, 2006).

I recommend what I call "breath control relaxation," because it's simple, direct, and is easily incorporated as a step toward personal meditation. It is worth knowing that the "gold standard" of relaxation induction is called "progressive relaxation," developed by cardiologist Edmond Jacobsen (1938) and refined by many others since. It involves a series of contrast exercises in which you tighten and then release muscles from head to toe. These exercises produce what is known as a deep muscle response. Sometimes people think that they can relax with a beer and a Sunday afternoon football game, and perhaps they can. But what we are after is "deep muscle relaxation" that emerges out of the training exercise with vigorous contrast episodes of tension and relaxation. This is a little different from kicking off your troubles by finding a good distraction.

The research supports progressive relaxation as the most effect induction procedure (cf. Conrad & Roth, 2007). The instructions go something like, "Clinch right fist, hold and study attention.... Now gently release the tension and let your hand relax .... Feel the contrast between tension and relaxation. . ." Another prominent type of relaxation involves "image" or "scene" induced relaxation. Here the person is instructed to envision themselves in a setting that has a historic association with relaxation and has a variety of positive stimulus attributes like a flowing brook, the sounds of birds and other wildlife, the warm sun, and a cooling breeze. "Why not combine progressive relaxation with image or scene presentation?" you might ask. Why not, indeed? And that's exactly what's done in producing scripts and sound recordings of relaxation exercises. While progressive relaxation is the gold standard, breath control relaxation is quite effective and is very easily integrated with meditation and suits our purposes just fine, as you shall see.

The beauty of using breath control relaxation and meditation together is that, in the same seated position, we can start with relaxation and then proceed directly into deeper quieting and contemplative stillness of meditation. The preparation for this relaxation procedure is as follows:

> Find a comfortable out-of-the-way place without distractions or attention from others.
>
> Place your feet flat on the floor and your head looking comfortably forward toward the horizon, or perhaps a location two or three meters away, while keeping your neck and shoulders in a comfortable position. It's not as important to be looking toward the horizon as it is to be comfortable.
>
> Find a comfortable seating position, preferably on a soft cushion, but without a backrest, where you can maintain yourself in a "free-balance." By free-balance I mean with your body not supported by chair back or cushions and your weight is distributed in a balanced position so that it takes little or no energy to sustain your posture.

What is described here will help to get you started on "first approximations" of the procedure. You may not get it just perfect the first time, but not to worry, or hurry, for that matter. More accurately, there is no perfect. Find what's comfortable for you and make whatever adjustments you need so it works for you. Feel free to move, stretch, shake your shoulders, shuffle your feet and so on, until it works for you.

Breathe Control Relaxation Exercise

> Be still and quiet. When you're ready, begin the following sequence:
>
> Without taking a long deep breath first, merely breathe normally and easily.
>
> Then, breathing through your nose, slowly exhale (again, no deep breath first) and continue to exhale, pushing as

Chapter 12 : Any Relief from the Stress?

much of the air out of your lungs as you comfortably can.

At the same time, hold your hands close to your chest with the tips of your fingertips just below your chin; press the palms of your hands together to help push the air out of your lungs. Your hands might resemble the "Lotus Blossom" or look like the classic gesture of Namaste or the gesture for "prayer."

Hold the air out, *but no longer than* 10 or 12 seconds. The point here is to stay within your comfort range, not in precision timing.

When you're ready to inhale, take at least two long, full, deep breaths before you speak. Nothing bad is likely to happen if you don't, it's just more comfortable to restore full oxygenation.

Let your body settle again into a relaxed, comfortable position and let your breathing normalize.

Repeat the process two or three times at a sitting. Do as many sittings as you wish during the course of the day.

It is unlikely that the full relaxation effect will occur the first time, and not necessarily by the 10th time either. Chances are it will take some skill development to get a start on the relaxation effect. This procedure will help us be relaxed, refreshed, and revitalized. The breath control relaxation exercise will not produce a sleepy, tired or sedating effect, but rather a deep sense of physical and mental relaxation.

Any exercise procedure known to humankind is subject to error or misunderstanding. In general, this one won't rip, rot, or tear. It's hard to imagine getting it mixed up in any way that could produce ill effects. I have seen it work for lots of people, but that doesn't mean that they got it on the first shot. Cut yourself a little slack and see what might work for you.

Check and Shake-Out.

"Check around and shake-out" is a kind of standard operating procedure in behavior management. Behavior runs on feedback and in order to get feedback we need to check to see what's going on.

Check for any tension that has crept into the usual places like your neck, shoulders, back or wherever it usually happens for you.

Gently shake out the tension, and let it dissipate.

Check your body position, try to remain in free-balance, without a backrest, by keeping your body in easy and relaxed equilibrium.

Remain mindful of yourself, your situation, your goals, and let yourself relax and settle.

Tuning up This Exercise.

As we become more familiar with this exercise we will find what works for you and what does not. As we move forward, just follow what works.

Also, as we become more comfortable with the exercise, we can exhale and hold the air out longer than 10 or 12 seconds, as is comfortable. Both pressure on the hands, arms, shoulders and breathing apparatus as well as full exhalation seem to be quite important to produce effectiveness.

Later in the day, after using this relaxation exercise, it might also be helpful to take a series of long full deep breaths. Make it a point to ventilate your lungs and enjoy the sensation of full oxygenation. While you're at it, you might find an out-of-the-way place, out of public attention and take some long full deep breaths and hold them for a comfortable time. The lore is that exhausting air from your lungs produces a negative change and that long, full breaths, including holding long, full, deep breaths provides a positive change to the system. In any case, the full, deep breaths will be invigorating.

Why should this relaxation exercise work?

Just like the progressive relaxation briefly described earlier, breath control relaxation involves a contrast between tension and relaxation. While it's automatic, breathing is an important job for our bodies. This exercise represents a departure from the usual, an interruption of routine and typical patterns, hence it is likely to provide a different effect. That is, we are accustomed to having at least partial lung inflation and in this exercise we push out a substantial amount of what is called "tidal" lung volume.

I have taught this exercise to hundreds and hundreds of clients over the years. My guess is it has worked well for something like 98% of the people who have tried it. The techniques that I have described here come from my own experience growing up in a family with parents who were mystics and being coached along in my early teens and beyond. I learned it as an exercise to relieve the symptoms of a common cold. My guess is is that it helps to relieve the common cold because it reduces stress and any kind of stress reduction, rest, energy boost is quite welcome when you have a cold bug.

There is another metaphor that applies to this relaxation exercise that I'll toss out for your consideration. There is a phenomenon known as the "dive reflex" (Breathology, 2012) in which people who fall overboard and are pulled down in cold water require less and less oxygen the deeper they go into the water as a result of increased water pressure on their bodies. I have wondered whether there's something happening in this exercise with the arm and shoulder pressure to push out the air and the reduced air volume in the lungs that capitalizes on this diving response. But, so much for my speculation, this is actually a question to be solved by research and I'll defer to the physiological psychologists or other biological investigators to handle this one.

Q & A

What if breath control relaxation does not work for me?

You might find that it will quickly pay off if you simply augment relaxation skills with some sort of progressive relaxation before you sit down to do breath control relaxation and merge into meditation.

What if I can't find a quiet place to practice this exercise?

I don't stand much on ceremony, and I suspect it would not benefit you to do so either. Just go ahead in a noisy place, with caution to ignore, "gate out," counteract the noise by using the skills that emerge as you practice.

What if things keep bothering me as I try to relax?

Not to worry. As you move forward into meditation you'll be able to quiet, settle, contemplate, be at peace, and find the path. Was it Edison who said that, "Genius is one percent inspiration, ninety-nine percent perspiration?" A little extra effort to get started will certainly payoff in the long run.

Chapter 13
Do I Need Meditation?
Meditation I

Overview

This chapter provides an introduction to meditation and a summary of health benefits of meditation based on the outcomes of research studies cited.

Quotations

Meditation is the gateway, through which you arrive to the world of freedom. *Remez Sasson*

Peace comes from within. Do not seek it without.
Look within, thou art the Buddha. *Buddha*

To understand the immeasurable, the mind must be extraordinarily quiet, still. *Jiddu Krishnamurti*

Meditation is not a way of making your mind quiet. It's a way of entering into the quiet that's already there – buried under the 50,000 thoughts the average person thinks every day. *Deepak Chopra*

What Is Meditation?

Here is a simple definition of meditation that might help us to all get started from the same place:

Meditation is a technique for working with the mind. If you think of the mind as a tool then the first step in putting it to use should be to examine it; then reflect on how it works and its possible uses; then put it to work as efficiently and effectively as you can. Meditation is a natural way of getting to know the mind so that we can investigate and understand how it works and then improve it through training. It takes a lot of practice to train the mind. (Meditation, 2014)

At its worst, learning meditation is a struggle, an onerous task we complete with little feedback or guidance, like trying to sail straight into the eye of the wind instead of making a proper tack, a bit off the wind. Or, perhaps we find ourselves in a kind of self-torture in which we accuse ourselves of being substandard, insufficient, unable to meet the mark, or perhaps things more ghastly.

Once we learn how to meditate, it is a fully relaxed and aware state of review, contemplation and evaluation, providing opportunity for examination of all things from the external world to the self. We will look at instructions for how to start the process of meditation in the next chapter.

Meditation is a means to transcend ourselves. It provides a comfortable easiness while going through the routines of daily life. It is a way to get from here to almost anywhere and back again without moving a muscle. It is an ancient skill known by women and men of all faiths, worldviews, persuasions, predilections, and ages. It is nothing we have to invent because it comes to us from the past millennia in which seekers have inherited or personally derived the method for entering into it.

What is Meditation Supposed to Do?

As we will see, there are many possible goals for meditation. Over the years practitioners have grown into a tradition, or defined for themselves the intended uses.

Chapter 13 : Do I need Meditation?

Jeff Halevy (2013) of *US News* points out that even the highly valued Transcendental Meditation (TM) does not seem to be terribly difficult:

> . . . the TM technique is relatively simple. One sits comfortably, closes his or her
> eyes, and repeats a mantra (in Sanskrit) without moving the lips or making a sound for about 20 minutes, two times a day. Yes, that's just about it. The only other crucial piece of information one must know to do the technique correctly is to not 'force' anything. That is, allow thoughts to come and go – and if one realizes he's stopped repeating the mantra in his head, to just gently come back to it.

Based on Halevy's description of TM, I think just about every style and tradition of meditation fits right in. When we come to what I'm recommending in the way of starting meditation practice, I will provide step-by-step instructions that are easy to follow. It won't be tough at all for us to jump straight into this elusive meditation thing.

Does Meditation Do What It's Supposed to?

I believe meditation is an important tool to develop in our lives:

> Meditation is considered to be safe for healthy people. . . . Individuals with existing mental or physical health conditions should speak with their health care providers prior to starting a meditative practice and make their meditation instructor aware of their condition. (Meditation-An Introduction, 2010)

I think it's fair to say that we have a procedure that is about as safe as getting out of bed in the morning. The next question is effectiveness, namely what can this mysterious pursuit do for us?

The following summary of research findings on meditation was provided by the David Lynch Foundation (Lynch, 2014). I have chosen to omit findings on "brain changes" because, as a psychologist, I always find them suspect. Ordinary behavioral outcomes are preferred because they are more easily understood and we can all tell what is relevant and what is at stake.

Benefits to Education

21% increase in high school graduation rate;

Education 133 (4): 495-500, 2013 10%

Improvement in test scores and GPA;

Education 131: 556–565, 2011

Increased attendance and decreased suspensions for high school students;

Health and Quality of Life Outcomes 1:10, 2003

Reduced ADHD symptoms and symptoms of other learning disorders;

Mind & Brain: The Journal of Psychiatry 2 (1): 73-81, 2011

Increased intelligence and creativity;

Intelligence 29: 419-440, 2001

40% Reduction in psychological distress, including stress, anxiety and depression; *American Journal of Hypertension* 22(12): 1326-1331, 2009

Reduction in teacher burnout and perceived stress; *Permanante Journal* 18 (1): 19-23, 2014

Benefits to Veterans

40-55% reduction in symptoms of PTSD and depression

Military Medicine 176 (6): 626-630, 2011;

42% Decrease in insomnia *Journal of Counseling and Development* 64: 212-215, 1985

25% Reduction in plasma cortisol levels;

Hormones and Behavior 10: 54–60, 1978

Decreased high blood pressure–on par with first-line antihypertensive *American Journal of Hypertension* 21: 310–316, 2008

47% reduced risk of cardiovascular-related mortality. *Circulation: Cardiovascular Quality and Outcomes* 5: 750-758, 2012

30% improvement in satisfaction with quality of life

Military Medicine 176 (6): 626-630, 2011

Benefits to Abused Women and Girls

Reduced flashbacks and bad memories

Military Medicine 176 (6): 626-630, 2011

Greater resistance to stress *Psychosomatic Medicine* 35: 341–349, 1973.

Twice the effectiveness of conventional approaches for reducing alcoholism and substance abuse. *Alcoholism Treatment Quarterly* 11: 13-87, 1994;

42% Decrease in insomnia *Journal of Counseling and Development* 64: 212-215, 1985.

Twice as effective as other relaxation techniques for decreasing trait anxiety. *Journal of Clinical Psychology* 45(6): 957–974, 1989.

Improved quality of life. *Military Medicine* 176 (6): 626-630, 2011

Other Findings:

The evidence . . . suggests that meditation training may effect positive changes in the multitasking practices of computer-based knowledge workers, and thus offers encouragement to those who would design workplace or technology interventions to take advantage of this possibility. (Levy, Wobbrock, Kaszniak, Ostergren, 2012)

Enhanced levels of mindfulness
Improvement on some indices of executive cognitive function.
Reduced levels of
  Depressive symptoms,
  Reflective rumination
  Negative affect (Chambers, Chuen-Yee &, Allen, 2008)

A Major Resource

We don't have to dress up in our finest Shaolin ceremonial robes in order to practice meditation; there is no particular need to think of meditation as only an ancient practice reserved for Buddhists. Nor should we avoid the use of meditation because it has some kind of trivial associations that make us feel silly, like old movies we have seen on TV. What we can identify from the above research findings is that we have a safe and effective practice that can serve us well for our personal needs in finding our path.

As a special resource, we must make every effort to use meditation wisely. It is a path from which we can find self-discovery and contentment. It will enable us to sort out the important from the trivial in our daily lives. It really can enable us to come to terms with

Chapter 13 : Do I need Meditation?

ourselves. If it sounds like a cure-all, like maybe meditation can do everything, it might be time to proceed with extreme caution. We may find our way to awakening and serenity through meditation but not reading, writing, and 'rithemetic. That is, meditation provides an avenue to perspective on our life and the world, not basic learning skills. Obviously, content areas like history, foreign languages, and all those gritty pieces we have to put together to understand our world don't come through meditation. Formal education and higher education are the better tracks. Of course there's nothing wrong with informal education, leisure reading, and special study in the areas of particular interest.

Q & A

If meditation is so good, why limit the scope of our use?

We are not talking magic here. Personally, I think it is remarkable what meditation can do for us and I suspect that the Buddha and many others before and since have understood the special quality of meditation. Coming to terms with ourselves is no small matter. But we will focus on using meditation to find our own peace and harmony. More on this later.

The two quotations, one saying, "Peace comes from within. . . ." and the other saying, "thou art the Buddha." seem a bit of a stretch. We're just getting started and there's something about being a Buddha. What is this stuff about, anyway?

Prince Siddhartha Gautama, a real person, was born around the year 563 BCE in Lumbini, in modern-day Nepal. "The Buddha," refers to "the enlightened one." The Buddhist tradition is very optimistic, hoping that we will always be on the lookout for enlightenment in others. As the story goes, when one walks about it's important to keep questioning whether the people we see in our lives are our newly "enlightened ones" and hence "the Buddha."

Life, Death and Spirituality

Chapter 14
Can I Wash this Junk Out of My Head?
Meditation II

Overview

Meditation skills can be used to seek resolution of personal issues and problems as well as move forward toward peace and harmony. We also look at how it is meditation might actually work.

Quotations

Drink deeply. Live in serenity and joy. *Buddha*

There is no need to go to India or anywhere else to find peace. You will find that deep place of silence right in your room, your garden or even your bathtub. *Elisabeth Kubler-Ross*

Pen and Paper

Taking notes during the process of meditation can greatly enhance the progress we can make in finding our way to peace and harmony. As we gather notes it will be a good idea to sort and compile them into a more usable order. With small sheets it's easy to gather them into topical stacks. As we move further along it's a good idea to be identifying themes in our lives. As we look through the themes it will be helpful to use them as further meditation topics, so that we can systematize our explorations. By looking at the topics and themes we might just develop insights about what's going on in our lives. As these components become part of our meditation topics we can begin to develop further emotional congruity with them and develop further understandings of ourselves. We can generate a personal plan for where we want to go in our lives. The natural step will be to check from time to time to see if we're getting there, or whether we need to make adjustments in our plans.

For note taking, small 4" x 6" sheets fit easily in a pocket or purse and the larger 8 ½ x 11 pages can accommodate larger themes. Jotting down notes on a pad within convenient reach is unlikely to be much of a problem. The notes we take are for our benefit. No, there's no homework to turn in, no quiz. The principle is to grab the thought before it gets away. It might be a good idea to identify and to track things like: what we still need to do after meditating; goals, aspirations, hurt feelings, life issues, head hassles etc. (I still have a list of life pressures and bothersome issues from 1973, when I was trying to finish graduate school. For me they are now astonishing mementoes of the past.)

Here are some examples of helpful note topics. If issues like job or career come up frequently, we have identified a theme. If concerns come up from time to time such as mom, dad, brother, sister, anger or fear, these are more themes. If awkward interpersonal exchanges that occurred had during the day, or after arriving home tired and one had to cope with other family members who were tired, and, irritable, perhaps that's another theme. In general, people, places and things are themes. Memories, especially bad ones, are themes. Feelings of joy and happiness or gratefulness are also themes. It's a really good idea to focus on themes that are "warm and fuzzy" as well as the troublesome, uncomfortable, wearing or irritating issues in our lives, as well. It's also good to have easy access to life issues that we will benefit from mastering.

Chapter 14 : Can I Wash this Junk Out of My Head?

Moving into Stillness

Meditation is a quiet and contemplative state of personal review and reflection, which has been practiced for millennia. In the US, Buddhism is perhaps the most widely known meditative tradition due to a book entitled, *The Way of Zen* (Watts, 1957), but there are many others. Meditation is a way to recharge the batteries, refresh oneself, without need of a beverage, and to reflect on important questions arising out of complicated situations. Some argue it is a basic requirement of living. There is a marvelous story about Westerners meeting with a Buddhist master asking the question, "Why meditate?" which produced the response, "Why eat?"

For our practice of meditation, find a quiet time and place away from the traffic of the household. Preferably it is a place with good seating and no distractions of its own. I sit still and meditate just about anywhere but my favored place at home is at the corner on the foot of the bed. It has good support, no back rest and it is high enough that my feet dangle in a restful fashion. We start with being still and using breath control relaxation exercise to initiate the quieting and stilling of the body and mind.

The process of meditation involves just turning over ideas, thoughts, feelings, experiences, our lives. We can look at our place in our social and physical worlds, by sorting of out who we are, what we're about, where we have come from and where we think we might be going. It can be a very substantial help in making sense out of ourselves, and who we want to become. Perhaps we might regard meditation as, thinking things over without really trying. It is a way to search for and discover hopes and fears, meanings, associations, forgotten experiences of the past, and sort out their impact on us today. Think of meditation as something like a really good night's sleep and a healthy breakfast for the spirit. Or perhaps it is like a cleansing hot shower before we ever thought we might need one. Whatever metaphor works best, I think we might find it is good for what ails us, especially before we become bothered or stressed.

Our practice of meditation is quite pragmatic. The focus is

indeed on settling down, coming to terms, experiencing and understanding the events of the day, but also problem identification, problem definition, tentative solutions and sequencing interventions. However, there are also the larger issues, like finding even greater calm and serenity than can be achieved with any kind of relaxation exercise. What we might find rather quickly is there is nothing terribly exotic, frightening or intimidating about meditation. It's really quite "homey," practical, routine, serviceable, useful, and fits like a soft slipper.

Free Balance Position

Seated in a free-balance position, (without our body supported by chair back or cushions and our weight is distributed in a balanced pose, so that it takes little or no energy to sustain our posture) we will let ourselves settle and be still. Let's close our eyes and free our thoughts, feelings and reactions allowing us to explore whatever comes along. There's nothing much to invoke, bring forth, avoid, suppress or hide from. The process is very natural and easy to achieve and maintain, except perhaps if a phone rings or a neighbor drops by.

The free-balance position is recommended for meditation, since it provides the opportunity for maintaining an active body connection while we reflect and contemplate. If we thought it was tough to stay awake in our last class at the end of the day, consider the awkwardness of starting meditation in a horizontal position only to discover later we nodded-off in the process. As we get comfortable with the free-balance position, it will enable us to maintain attention, awareness, presence, mindfulness, and a contemplative attitude. There are all sorts of notions about how to sit and how to meditate, but I think we want to take these recommendations in moderation. About placement of the arms and hands, the position I favor is to rest the wrists on the thighs, while placing the thumb, first and second fingers together. This leaves two fingers free, but they don't seem to get confused or wander about, so

Chapter 14 : Can I Wash this Junk Out of My Head?

not to worry. We can rearrange ourselves in a manner that is most comfortable for us.

As we relax, let the thoughts, feelings and the mental images that show up drift through our heads. No need to push or pull them, start or stop them or be scared by them or anything much at all. As they come through, just observe in a fully relaxed, dispassionate, spectator fashion. As with all new things, it takes a while to get used to the routine. Let's give ourselves a chance. There's no urgency, there is nothing we will miss out on, nor do we have to be the first one on the block to do meditation. It is hard to imagine that there are unusual risks or dangers for us here. Well, what if we have bad dreams when we sleep? We can easily get the idea. These are clearly "non-events" and we just get on with it.

Easy Themes

We are now ready to start this exotic meditation thing, and hence the dilemma of themes, concerns, topics, or issues upon which to meditate. Not to worry! As we sit in the free-balance position, at rest, open to experience, nature will provide plenty of opportunities. Events of the day, life hassles, decisions facing us, and people of our lives, who are generous, kind and loving, as well as the people of our lives who are not so kind or generous, might come into our thoughts. Be as an observer of the stream of thoughts, feelings, ideas, conflicts, as they wash through in a totally disorderly fashion. The strategy is to simply let it all happen without any concern about organizing events or disapproving of some of the ideas and images that stream by; simply accept all in a dispassionate review of the flow of material that emerges. We don't allow trivial issues to prevent us from making sense out of our experience.

What we're looking for is an opportunity to see, hear, think and feel our own lives. It's important to understand how the pieces of our experience go together to produce our lives and to emerge with some understanding of who we are and what we are about. A major goal is to understand, our history, challenges, opportunities and what we might do to make positive changes in our life trajectory. There is a good intuitive handle for this idea and the notion offered by Carkhuff and Berenson (1967) namely, "dynamic self-understanding." What they are saying is, we need to understand ourselves in our lives, in our families, in our history, in the multiple cross pressures of the life we live, our past and our present.

The most critical meditation theme is us, that is to say, it is ourselves. If we focus on dynamic self-understanding, all the rest will follow. We want to look at ourselves in our world, as best we can understand it at the time. Energized by focusing on who we are and how we got to be where we are, we can begin to come to some understanding of what we are about. It's probably important to recognize that such understandings are not achieved in a single trial. It's not like we can do that in just a single five or fifty-minute meditation experience. In our meditation and in our lives, in our world action every day, we need to understand, and then to re-understand our history, ourselves, the challenges and the opportunities we face and what we might do to maximize our own personal-growth potential.

Although it might sound a little challenging, each step we take provides its own reward and moves us on to the next steps. I'm reminded of a marvelous high school mathematics teacher who talked about the process of completing our homework assignment. Mr. Archie Elliott pointed out, when we find the solution for the first problem in the assignment, we will be so buoyed-up, excited, and energized by the experience that we will easily move on to the next problem, and the next until we have finished the entire assignment. To put it another way, once we get to the experience of, "Holy-mackerel, this actually works!" we can easily go forward with great gusto.

Similarly, as we heed natural feedback and learn the skills, we will be propelled forward with delight and ready to take on the next challenge.

Chapter 14 : Can I Wash this Junk Out of My Head?

Q & A

How will I know if I am meditating correctly?

There is not just one way to meditate. There are many different traditions and many personal styles. There is plenty of latitude for personal preferences and exploration.

Could I just be wasting my time doing this?

We learn by feedback and our minds and bodies will not let us down. There will be plenty of cues and prompts so that we can determine what works and what does not.

Chapter 15
Should I Keep on Scrubbing?
Meditation III

Overview

We consider meditation in more detail and provide some help for identifying personal issues and life themes to focus on.

Quotations

There are two mistakes one can make along the road to truth... not going all the way, and not starting. *Buddha*

Meditation is a time to focus, train the mind, and bring it to stillness. It is not a time to rest and relax. *Darren Main*

Meditate. Live purely. Be quiet. Do your work with mastery. Like the moon, come out from behind the clouds.... Shine! *Buddha*

Next Steps

Some meditative traditions use devices to increase concentration; there are strategies like, looking into an open fire or a lighted candle, ringing a bell or gong, or watching some swinging object to help focus attention to help the process to go more smoothly. It would certainly not be out of the way to try any of these devices. Who knows, there might be something that might be helpful here. However, from my experience these add-ons don't make much difference. It is more like learning to ride a bicycle. What's needed is time on-task in a pleasantly relaxed state with a readiness to enjoy the process.

On the question of how long to meditate, the general principle is to do what works best for us. It might be a good idea to set aside a special time each day. Try a few minutes and then take a break to do something else. Work up to a comfortable length of time that is suitable for us and our needs. If there is an hour available or half an hour or even a quarter of an hour, meditation is still a good investment in our future. As we get more experienced we can use not only that reserved time, but also five, ten or twenty minutes whenever it fits into our schedule. Like eating, sleeping, or walking, we word want to adjust our activity level to suit our needs. This is a trial and error process and it's hard to imagine that anything could go wrong while we're finding what fits for us. It's also important to use available and convenient times that fit into our daily schedule, rather than becoming a slave to meditation.

Distractions are everywhere and are virtually guaranteed as we start meditative practice. Just ignore them and go on as we would with any other activity. Since we may be unable to escape some distractions, try focusing on them intensely, one at a time, like dealing with the debris that might float through our minds. There is a good chance they will wash away and dissipate. Nonsensical, silly or tangential thoughts are all part of the process and should be ignored. Meditation isn't disrupted by distractions. Rather, meditation will help us focus our thoughts, reflections, recollections and images. Allow the thoughts to drift through and let the trivial distracting ones dissipate and vanish.

What if we have uncomfortable thoughts when we meditate instead of peacefulness and equanimity? As we've seen, try focusing

Chapter 15 : Should I Keep on Scrubbing?

on the unpleasant thoughts. The intuitive notion is, we might run but we can't escape. There's nothing to lose by focusing on them, exploring their contents, turning over their meanings, and even getting hold of the bad stuff. My bet is that they will soon dissipate, exhaust and be gone.

The notion of letting intrusion exhaust and dissipate is counterintuitive, since it would be easy to buy into the notions of concentrating and controlling. Instead of attempting to control, simply let more unplanned thoughts and feelings just happen. We are not so much talking about some sort of willpower as we are washing out the debris. In order for that to happen, we may need both more debris and more washing-water. We need a whole lot less clutching and a whole lot more "going with the flow."

What's needed is time-on-task focus and making a substantial, sustained effort over a reasonable time. Also, we need to relax more, rather than grit our teeth to enhance our willpower. I think we need to dismiss any intimidating ideas that somehow say it's us and we just can't do it. Cleansing meditation isn't the sort of thing we can make happen. We need to let it happen. When it does, enjoy the cleansing-glow but also be ready with our notepad so that we may return to the major themes later.

For our purposes, meditation is a very ordinary process, like eating, sleeping, walking or sitting in the shade on a hot summer day. I don't find it exalting, making me a special person, or spooky, making it a scary adventure. By the same token, I don't find it sacrosanct either. Some people describe special, altered states of consciousness emerging from meditation. My experience is there is an even deeper sense of relaxation and mental cleansing in meditation than there is in any type of relaxation exercises and a kind of comfort that is many times stronger.

When events, personal issues, and relationships are persistently troubling they come back into our thoughts repeatedly. Whether we are in a meditative state, or simply in a quiet place where we can reflect, it may help to simply ask ourselves a question like, "What is it?" or better yet, make a personal statement like, "I wonder what it is." If we can stay sufficiently relaxed and attentive, we may get an answer. If we don't, not to worry, it is likely to come along as we get more comfortable. The notion here is to tune into ourselves, focus on our experience, and begin to put into words what it is that ails us. It surely doesn't happen accidentally or quickly. It's worthwhile to be patient. When ideas, insights or understandings come through, be sure to note them for follow-up.

Will meditation take us to joy everlasting? Will we be disappointed if we don't get exactly what we wanted from it? Can we collect on a guarantee? Unlikely. Meditation is a skill and a tool, a means to go forward in our lives.

Quick Recap of Meditation

> Relax
> Close your eyes
> Start with breath control relaxation
> Be patient
>
> Let anything and everything drift past whenever it wants to:

Thoughts
Images
Confusion
Feelings
Drifting
Incomprehensible events
Whatever is our worst fear

> We can also allow things to happen that we want to happen:

Dispassionate self-observation
Experiencing, feeling
Serenity, stillness
Composure, refreshment

Chapter 15 : Should I Keep on Scrubbing?

Savoring, relishing
Expanding, globalizing
Perceiving, understanding, insight
Tolerance, forgiveness, compassion
Self-acceptance

Let's make up our minds in advance that when distracting thought happen while meditating, we will simply list the problem, concern or life issue on our follow up agenda and take it up at another time. The possibilities might be feelings of anger or resentment, or bad memories from the past. Or, anticipation of a positive event. In the long run, all of these issues are grist for the mill. We just want to take them up when we are comfortable managing them, not before. If it is scary or really uncomfortable, go back to relaxation and let it go.

More on Concentration

It seems to me, the standard lore on meditation is, "You have to focus your concentration in order to reap the full benefit from the practice." As indicated above (in this chapter), one of the ways meditation can help us is by enhancing our concentration. This occurs by simply exhausting the junk thoughts that come into our heads. If meditation can help us with concentration, we don't need to have focused, high levels of concentration from the start to make it work for us. Meditation (thought, contemplation, deliberation, reflection) is a psychological process like many others and can be understood in relation to a model of how behavior works. The most direct example is anxiety and especially anxiety with panic. (cf. Clark & Beck (2011). On interview, people describe rising levels of fretfulness that comes to a maximum and then plateaus. By helping them to identify what is actually happening to them rather than concluding it is the worst fears of their experience, they can be assisted to allow the internal experience to stop building, dissipate and exhaust. While this might be an uncomfortable process, it's important to remember that it can't hurt us. As we have discussed, while meditating, just relax, be a spectator and observe what is happening. No need to struggle with the experience or try to redirect it. The junk in our head will dissipate, exhaust, and tier-out. While it fades away, we can easily select the topics we choose and focus on them.

Figure 7.1, below, illustrates what happens. As we observe our own situation, the junk in our heads increases dramatically, as we pay attention to it. As we ignore it and remind ourselves not to pay any attention to this debris, it fades away showing occasional recurrences from time to time, as if to catch us unaware. Since we know better than to pay attention to it the junk, it continues to dissipate and fade away. The figure displays the internal experience we have during this process, called Subjective Units of Discomfort (SUDS)

Figure 15.1

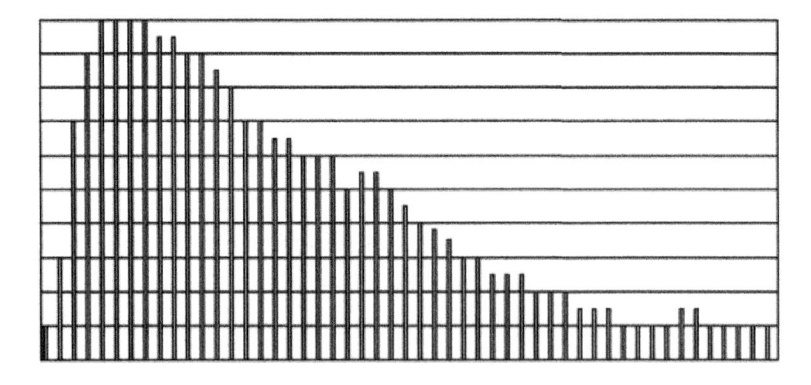

Time

Meditation helps to clear our heads, enables concentration and allows us to pick and choose our themes and topics of focus. The excessive direction to concentrate in order to meditate is not much help and is a distraction or hindrance. Just be patient and follow your nose.

Chapter 15 : Should I Keep on Scrubbing?

Why are We Meditating, Anyway?

Meditation is an ancient practice which allows us to go into a dramatically relaxed and contemplative state which enhances our ability to concentrate on wheat and discard chaff. Down through history people have used meditation because it worked for them for religious, spiritual, mystical and personal goals. We may use it for our own purposes, regardless of what it is advocated by others.

We can use meditation to clear and refresh our minds and bodies. Notice that this book has a methods section, but that only relaxation and meditation are considered here. These skills plus the knowledge base we bring to our effort are what we need. We can live our lives, face an ambiguous and uncertain future and come to the ending of life with a sense of serenity, peace and harmony, supported by these resources.

For Future Reference

As we move along with relaxation and meditation practices, they will become familiar old friends. As they do, we can use the feedback and behavioral cues that nature provides, just like we do in the rest of our lives, to guide us in the right direction. One of the things we're likely to be aware of is changes in our breathing. In particular, if our breathing becomes shorter and shallower while we're meditating. Breathing changes may indicate a topic or life issue that has some emotional impact, which might be a good candidate for a list to be retrieved again in the near future. Going forward, we can sort out what it's about for us. Carl Rogers (1961), talks about organismic trusting, by which he means trusting our body and ourselves to provide accurate feedback. We become increasingly aware of it as we move forward with relaxation and meditation. Nature gives us good cues and prompts that we can follow in order to get where we are going.

Additionally, notes taken in the process of meditation can help us with our side of the bargain. What is needed is to identify themes in our lives and work out the potholes and bumps on our path. As we compile our list of issues, we need to bring them to our meditation time. As we generate more experience and the mist begins to clear, spend a few minutes, or as long as it takes, to turn over these problems, issues or themes one by one. This will be an important beginning for the processes of problem identification and problem solving in our lives and coming to terms with the realities of our situation. As our skills are further developed, we can regularly expand our meditation to include more items from our list. As we expand our capabilities in this area, we might want to develop, some sort of personal tracking system to see when we begin reviewing an item in our meditation, and when we conclude that it is sufficiently resolved to discontinue it and move forward.

Good hunting and good meditating!

Q & A

What if somebody asks what I'm doing sitting alone in the light, or the dark?

From time to time we all do some things that other people question. Handle it like you would any other situation. If you *want* to explain, feel free. Just be aware that it might take substantial background information before what you're doing would really be understandable to them.

What if we feel uncomfortable, or have body aches while meditating?

We can feel free to change anything that makes us physically or emotionally uncomfortable. It's not like meditation is a pre-arranged trip with no variations or course changes. We can adjust our posture, breathing, foot position, or anything else. I find it important to check-and-shake-out, as described above. A little shake of the shoulders to brush away some tension, repositioning of the feet or knees, arms, etc. never seems to do any harm. We can stretch, get up, walk around, or whatever we want, to make things work better for our own personal style.

Chapter 15 : Should I Keep on Scrubbing?

What if we don't get comfortable doing meditation?

Give it a substantial try. If we conclude that it's really not for us, it still might be helpful to look over the rest of the line of argument in this book. Equipped with the concepts and skills, the breath control relaxation exercise or even an audio disc of progressive relaxation could be very helpful until meditation feels more comfortable.

Chapter 16
Isn't Meditation just Meditation?
Meditation IV

Overview

Next is a review of some goals of meditation to find out where we fit in the larger scheme of things and then consider possible mechanisms by which meditation might work.

Quotations

Be still, quiet and patient. There is only you. How can there be a distance between you and you? *Jac O'Keeffe*

Delight in mediation and solitude. Compose yourself, be happy. You are a seeker. *Buddha*

The world is full of people looking for spectacular happiness while they snub contentment. *Doug Larson*

Meditation Goals

We will be using the fundamental skill of meditation to further our goals of coping with life and death and finding peace and harmony. The Buddhist meditative tradition, among others, uses the same practice for much different goals, often referred to as awakening, enlightenment, or the path to Nirvana. Although we're looking for a personal tune-up to make sure that our lives are running along smoothly, other goals are quite possible.

The conceptual model used in in this book is a practical, utilitarian and limited-goal concept. What we're after is to even out the bumps and potholes of our lives, as well as deal with angst and the fear of death. We have drawn on the major meditative traditions to get insight into what meditation is, how it works and how it might be applicable to our needs. We have the good fortune of finding a technology available "off the shelf." We have not had to invent anything new, complicated or untried. We simply adapted an existing practice. Our goals will be limited to our present needs, as above. We also look at some of what I learned to do as a young man and have practiced, over the years, as it suited me.

As we have seen, various religious traditions have groups within them that use meditation in a daily practice. I have a particular affinity for the Buddhists and their meditative practice. They are a mainline meditative tradition and one of the world's major thought traditions. That is, it's not merely small groups within the Buddhists, or an incidental component of their practice, but a fundamental part of their teachings and a major tool to reach their goals. Their goal is awakening, enlightenment or Nirvana, a state of contentment or bliss, which is the final goal state of Buddhist meditative practice (Nirvana, 2013). They are not content with our limited goals, but rather pursue their religion-philosophy to its prescribed goal of oneness or selflessness. (cf. Landaw, Bodian and Buhnemann, 2011). Please note that this is a reference book with allusions to various other parts of the text and with parenthetical commentaries along the way:

Finding the Common Threads in Buddhist Enlightenment

The experience of enlightenment, though described slightly differently and approached by somewhat different means, bears notable similarities from tradition to tradition.

Enlightenment consistently signals the end of the illusion of separation

Chapter 16 : Isn't Meditation just Meditation?

Notice we said illusion because Buddhism teaches that, rather than doing away with separation, you awaken to the fact that it never existed to begin with. When you're enlightened, you no longer identify yourself as a distinct, isolated somebody inside your body or head confronted by a world of separate objects and others. Instead, you view reality as one continuous and interdependent whole - whether this reality consists of no-self, emptiness, true nature, mind, consciousness, or the ever-changing flux of phenomena. At a relative level, of course, you still know the difference between your body and your neighbor's body, lock your keys in your car at the worst possible time, pay the bills (or forget to pay them), and kiss your children (not someone else's) good-night. (cf. . Landaw, Bodian and Buhnemann, 2011)

To put it in a very ordinary way, the Buddhists are eager to find their place in the cosmos and have developed a variety of powerful strategies to get there.

Mechanics

We start with breath control relaxation to settle our bodies and minds down substantially. Use the seated, free balance position as described earlier. As we begin to settle in and feel comfortable, we make the natural bridge into meditation without even changing chairs. We simply discontinue the breath exercise and begin observing what is happening with your thoughts.

With practice, meditation involves a very serene physical and mental state, but it could also focus on life situations that have been stressful or as yet unresolved. That is, this meditation practice is about us, it involves us because it is of us, who we are, what we're about, how our world works for us, or perhaps, how it doesn't work for us. Here-in lies the opportunity. If we can get at some of our life issues, some of our vulnerabilities, and some of our idiosyncrasies, so much the better. Coming to terms with who we are, what we are about, while we are in a relaxed state could not do us much harm.

A psychological procedure called desensitization of phobia is

Life, Death and Spirituality

a treatment which comes to us through behavioral psychology. It involves developing a very strong relationship with the therapist, who assists in inducing a relaxed state and then helps to sort out and reduce our reactivity to emotionally provocative or difficult issues in our life.

Did any of the many meditative traditions anticipate behavioral psychology and relaxation training or desensitization treatment? I don't think so. But they simply followed their noses, looking for nature's cues and prompts which emerge in a relaxed and contemplative state. They found their way to an impressive practice that can be learned with coaching and effort. Like our forbearers of the various meditative traditions, most of what we need to do in order to get this to work for us is to follow the cues that nature provides and do what produces the desired outcomes.

Just as in the question of how breath-control relaxation works (Ch. 11), a series of well-designed studies will be required to really get at the mechanisms that operate in meditation. This is an empirical question, the kind that can only be resolved by experimental studies. Until studies become available, here is my conceptual model of how it might work.

Having practiced breath control relaxation in the free balance position, the free balance position itself may produce behavioral cues (stimuli) associated with a relaxed state. Just as the sight of a roller coaster may give us the feeling of a queasy stomach because of visual cues, the free balance position will begin to elicit a relaxed and contemplative state. From the free balance position, it's a natural step to review life concerns, problems and fears in the meditative state.

If we look carefully, there are important similarities between meditative states and the psychotherapeutic process. What we are looking at here is a kind of analogous situation between personal meditation, individual psychotherapy or group psychotherapy. The goal of our meditation is to achieve an emotional and mental cleansing that helps us make sense out of our lives and come to terms with our situation. The goals of psychotherapy are not very different.

Chapter 16 : Isn't Meditation just Meditation?

Additionally, the relaxed and reflective state of both procedures is likely to be the major mechanism (source of gain) by which the person achieves recovery. While meditation and psychotherapy seem to have very similar goals and work in very similar ways, meditation is no substitute for psychotherapy, in which there is a high level of partnership between client and therapist.

In any comparison of meditation and psychotherapy, the obvious objection is, where's the therapist? Millions and millions of people never seek psychotherapeutic help. Did they grow up in a life experience that prevented the development of widely occurring personal problems? If they did develop some sort of emotional vulnerabilities, idiosyncrasies or struggles, did they already have the benefit of skills that would help them find their own way out? I think the answer is "yes" in both cases. However, we need to sharpen the focus here. Problem solving and communication, and what are called stress inoculation skills, have been demonstrated to be very powerful in helping people move forward in their lives (cf. Meichenbaum, 2007). At its simplest, stress inoculation allows the person to anticipate future situations that are likely to be difficult. By inducing relaxation and presenting the scene in the form of images, the therapist can assist the person in reducing the stress they experience. When the real life situation comes along, they are more prepared. Again, we are looking for the conceptual similarities between practices rather than any kind of direct identity between them.

I had the good fortune of teaching an introduction to psychology section in which a brave student stood up in a large lecture hall and described how he had listed a series of his life problems, made sure to get really relaxed and considered them one by one. He repeated this procedure several times over the course of some weeks. He reported that he found himself recovering, even more than he had expected. As I pointed out to our class, he had derived (developed, independently invented) a personal method of desensitization that would have inspired even pioneers in the field

The second example comes from a friend who went through a

protracted divorce fight in which he was repeatedly threatened with jail for some wrong-doing he was unable to figure out. He explained that it was scary at first, but as he thought it over, it occurred to him there was some action he could take to deal with the threat. He went to a local jail, met the jailer, and explained his situation. He requested the opportunity to spend a few minutes sitting in one of the vacant cells. While the keeper of the keys thought it was a little strange, he didn't see it as an unreasonable request and made it possible for my friend to step in. Shortly afterward, he came out, expressed his appreciation and went on his way. A formal treatment procedure that would incorporate what he did for himself would be called "in-vivo desensitization." That is, it was an in-life experience in which he, in a relaxed state, voluntarily placed himself in the dreaded pokey. He reported that afterwards he was able to handle the threats of jail with much greater serenity.

Q & A

Are you telling us, your readers, we somehow can't use meditation for larger purposes? You have referred to what we're doing as a limited set of goals. Isn't there something wrong with that?

No, there is nothing wrong with specific and limited goals. We are setting ourselves more limited goals than the various meditative traditions, since we seek to cope with our world in peace and harmony. A silly example is digging fencepost holes in the backyard. We are not likely to be able to put in a pump and get crude oil out of the holes but maybe the fence will stay up for a while.

Is there any reason we cannot use our meditation skills for the purpose of awakening or enlightenment?

Sure you can. Go right ahead. As we noted, this is a different goal from what we set for ourselves at the outset, but there's no reason the skills you are developing can't work for these broader purposes.

Chapter 17
How could Meditation Actually Work?
Meditation V

Overview

We look at events occurring across thousands of years to understand the lineage of meditation and modern behavioral psychology.

Quotations

Meditation is painful in the beginning, but it bestows immortal Bliss and supreme joy in the end. *Swami Sivananda*

Take the time to come home to yourself every day. *Robin Casarjean*

As meditation deepens, compulsions, cravings and fits of emotion begin to lose their power to dictate our behavior. *Eknath Easwaran*

Models

Let's look at some anecdotes that may serve as models to help us understand how behavior change has been managed and understood over the years.

Life, Death and Spirituality

In *The Ascent of Man*, Jacob Bronowski (1974) provides a tour of caves of primitive man in Altamira, Spain, which contain paintings of the hunter's encounter with dangerous wild game animals. These caves were first painted 11,000 to 19,000 years ago (Koeller, 1996). Brawnowski explains that the caves have no artifacts of food, animal skins or other remnants that would indicate they were used as living quarters. He offers what he calls a personal view:

> I think that the power that we see expressed here for the first time is the power of anticipation, the forward-looking imagination. In these paintings the hunter was made familiar with dangers which he knew he had to face, but to which he had not yet come. When the hunter was brought here into the secret dark and the light was suddenly flashed on the pictures he saw the bison as he would have to face him. He saw the running deer, he saw the turning boar. And he felt alone with them as he would in the hunt. The moment of fear was made present to him, his spear-arm flexed with an experience which he would have and which he needed not to be afraid of. The painter had frozen the moment of fear, and the hunter entered it through the painting as if through an air-lock
>
> . . . . for the hunter, I suggest they were a peep-hole into the future, he looked ahead. In either direction the cave paintings act as a kind of telescope tube of the imagination. They direct the mind from what is seen to what can be inferred or conjectured.

Bronowski (1974) is arguing that the prospective hunter is given the opportunity to place himself into the experience of the climax of the hunt before going on his quest. It is that crucial moment of the kill for which the hunter must prepare himself. In the case of large and potentially dangerous animals, the hunter is vulnerable to the prey and substantial composure is required to face

Chapter 17 : How Could Meditation Actually Work?

and confront it. By so doing, the hunters have the opportunity to calm their emotions and ready themselves for the crucial encounter of "kill or be killed." I think the theme here is preparation or inner peace.

In a very different example, Buddha (563 BCE - 483 BCE) focuses on personal experiencing and oneness and admonishes us to look for our peace within ourselves. Finding peace and enlightenment inside is an explicit message with substantial prompting to pursue this avenue.

Peace comes from within. Do not seek it without. *Buddha*

I'm struck that while pursuing an inner experience of serenity we are in effect realigning ourselves with the external natural world in which we live. Stillness, reflection and meditation bring a sense of peace that seems to emerge from washing the junk out of our heads.

> It is better to conquer yourself than to win a thousand battles. Then the victory is yours. It cannot be taken from you, not by angels or by demons, heaven or Hell. *Buddha*

While we are finding ourselves we are adapting to the realities of the natural world. By my lights, "to conquer yourself" is to come to terms, make sense out of and adapting to the natural world.

Now let's fast-forward a few thousand years, or so. Psychological notions of dealing with our behavior and emotional states did not arrive much before the 1920s or 1930s. They involve adaptation to fear-provoking stimuli. The clearest example is to encourage a water phobic child to play on the beach near the water without any attempt to force them into even the shallow water nearby. Depending on the size of the child and the nature of their play they will begin to adapt to the environment. As they get comfortable with the shore they may have some more interest in the edge of the water, perhaps putting their feet into it. This is the beginning of the adaptation or "getting used to it." The notion is that play is relaxing and encourages personal exploration. As the youngster adapts to the situation, they feel more comfortable exploring and the water's edge and it becomes the most fun thing in sight. (cf. http://www.helpguide.org/articles/anxiety/phobias-and-fears.htm)

As we have already seen (Ch. 11) more focused approaches to producing the relaxation response and opportunities to present increasingly challenging stimuli can move this process along substantially. We have discussed relaxation training and desensitization of phobia, talking about them as if they were quite ordinary. Perhaps they are at this point in time, but it took some years for concepts and procedures to be developed from humble beginnings, like adapting to the shore, the water's edge and finally the water.

Bronowski's (1974) interpretation of the cave paintings is quite persuasive to me. What comes through is that psychology, as a science of behavior, has an astonishing, intuitively understandable heritage of folk wisdom. Notice also that the Buddha might be seen as a powerful thinker who really understood human behavior.

These three examples do not merely represent an artistic expression or a prophet's prescriptive approach to living, or a fledgling science offering practical recommendations for ordinary life problems, but rather a behavior management approach of making ourselves right with the natural world. These strategies have a long and courageous heritage that should not surprise us. I find it quite encouraging that ancient cave dwellers, Buddha and early psychology researchers identified practical needs that could be addressed by strategies they could intuit from which to derive solutions. By self-observation the people who tried the remedies could judge their effectiveness and so can we. There would seem to be little need to accept behavior change principles with deference to authority or on some misplaced faith. Testing out such notions is something like testing new foods. It is only good if it is tasty to you.

Chapter 17 : How Could Meditation Actually Work?

Q & A

Wait a second! How do these three developments relate to one another, cave paintings, teachings of the Buddha and early developments in behavioral psychology?

It is true that these threads do not seem to have been connected before. They were not only thousands of years apart but also continents apart. While there is little chance they influenced one another, they have a powerful continuity. Ancient peoples were not dummies; to the contrary, here we see marvelous insights. We can see a powerful convergence of ideas that help to validate the developments of recent thinking.

Is that all there is? Is that all we get about meditation? As you pointed out, other authors write books about meditation. Are you just giving us short shrift?

We talked, now many times about following our noses, about the problem of making a very ordinary practice into a mysterious process and about the practicalities of meditation. It is surely OK to search websites or read books about it, but perhaps you may want to get on with the program.

Life, Death and Spirituality

Chapter 18
Fearless Being and Becoming?
Oneness

Overview

Two simple models are offered to illustrate how we function in our daily lives and to exemplify how we might move forward toward our goals. We are already doing a lot of what we need to do, but some fine-tuning would be helpful, to move us along our path in a more effective manner.

Fearlessness

No one knows the future. Hence, we live in a world of ambiguity and uncertainty. Gathering some sort of peace and harmony helps to take the edge off. Fear of harmful, risky or dangerous situations, like a rattlesnake den, is a good thing because we are more likely to keep a safe distance. Even with all of our cooperative relationships there is still the dilemma of who will get the next promotion, adding competition to the reality of our situation. And so we come to the question, in a world of high levels of uncertainty and stress, where could we look to find some modicum of peace and harmony? I have argued that looking to some external personal God is not a reasonable way to achieve personal harmony. We need to look into ourselves. Here's a thought exercise to help demonstrate the principle:

Who is merely mortal and has any of the following?
- Insecurity
- Personal conflicts
- Anxiety, Apprehension
- Angst, Torment
- *Ennui*, Dissatisfaction
- Preoccupations
- Bad memories
- Moodiness

Who needs to track and figure things out to get through the day, week, year and might benefit from the following tools and strategies?
- Notepad- Pocket / Purse
- Checklists
- Task analysis
- Resource inventory
- Problem identification
- Problem definition
- Problem solving
- Life planning

Answer? We all do! The place to resolve our disharmonies is within ourselves. Since we all have the foibles of mere mortality, we need to have formal or informal tools to get through our lives. How can we make our lives work better for us? My answer is, it won't be too tough because, most of us already do these things intuitively and naturally. We are creatures with good resources but also substantial limitations. Unless we want to live on the edge, we need to take our limitations into account and identify steps that will compensate for them.

Fearlessness? Why should it matter? It is not at all that we are "tough guys" who endure any pain or hardship. Couldn't we just clench our teeth and go forward, no matter what? Not a good idea.

Chapter 18 : Fearless Being and Becoming?

Rather, fear, and in particular anxiety, when it is extreme, can be both disabling and produce adverse consequences. This is because anxiety is uncomfortable we naturally look for anxiety reduction. Our behavior can be adversely shaped by any event, no matter how useless, self-defeating or in-harmonious, which provides some sort of anxiety reduction.

An explanation is offered by the two-factor theory of learning (Mowrer, 1956), but maybe the idea is best conveyed using an ordinary example. A man walks home on a familiar route each day, where he passes a house with a friendly dog, which he pets. One day either he or the dog takes a misstep and he stands on the foot of the dog producing sharp pain and a bite on his ankle by a frightened and defensive dog. A dog with which he was once friendly has produced a painful bite on his ankle, which did not break the skin.

The man is now very guarded, cautious and anxious about the dog. He changes his route to and from home to avoid the dog. Every time he gets even a glimpse of the dog he feels the intense anxiety and walks the other way. In short, the man has developed an avoidance reaction. That is, he stays clear of the dog and goes the other way at the first glimpse of the formerly friendly dog. Anxiety and fear of the dog are likely to remain unresolved as long as he's unable to approach the dog. That's why it's called avoidance. These fearful reactions are usually resolved with relaxation and desensitization to the fear provoking stimulus. But without some kind of intervention, there is little likelihood of resolution since the man is unable to be in visual range, much less anywhere near close to the dog.

Fearlessness is not a reasonable goal for us any more than inability to feel pain. Fear and pain are important signals that we count on to keep us safe from danger. Rather than fearlessness we are looking for mindfulness and oneness. Serenity, relaxation and harmony are important objectives because they can help to inoculate us from unhealthy behaviors emerging out of ordinary efforts to reduce anxiety. Serenity and stillness are good waypoints on our path to peace and harmony. We are now in the process of accumulating the skills with which to induce them, particularly in the form of relaxation and meditation.

Life tasks and opportunities.

As we settle ourselves in our everyday lives, as well as cope with the episodic fear of ultimate death, we have it within our grasp to live a full and enjoyable life. But what does it take to be fully engaged in our lives? I argue there are several functions we need to deal with both in the moment and over time. Below are some brief sketches of what these functions are about.

Mindfulness. The notion of mindfulness is the idea of being fully involved and attentive to our situation. Major emphasis on mindfulness is found in both the Buddhists (cf. Landaw, Bodian and Buhnemann, 2011) and psychology literature (cf. Linehan, 1993). It enables us to increase a personal presence and awareness of our circumstance. Mindfulness places us in the moment of the activities that we are engaged in just then. It enables us to experience our world fully, without being preoccupied with events of the past or expectations of the future. Concentrating on the current task is necessary for successful completion of that task but also enables us to tune into tasks as a necessary part of sustaining ourselves in our world. But it's worth remembering that mindfulness isn't everything. There are many other functions to which we need to attend to maintain ourselves in our world.

Reflection. Complementary to mindfulness we need to reflect, reconsider, analyze, understand the implications of events in our lives. Thoughts and ideas are important to our ability to move forward in our lives and developing alternative understandings is a critical piece of this process. The Buddha points out that what we think we become. We need to fully be present in our world but also fully reconsider, put into perspective, analyze and make sense of our life experiences.

Chapter 18 : Fearless Being and Becoming?

Being. As we become mindful, we can fully be ourselves and experience who we are. It helps to take the advice of the rock group, Rare Earth, and "...celebrate another day of livin'." Even when life is good we need to recharge our batteries, live to the fullest to repair and heal. Maybe this is in the form of taking in the ballgame or visiting with good friends, or tinkering with some ongoing hobby or project. Whatever it is that works for savoring, enjoying, and diverging, have great power to help us to re-create ourselves. These are revitalizing functions that substantially contribute to the richness of our life experience.

Becoming. We also need to be able to grow, change and develop in order to adapt to new circumstances as we experience them. That is, as we can, celebrate who we are and fully experience ourselves in the moment. We also want to maintain flexibility, and move forward in our lives, and continue to re-make ourselves in the direction of our personal ideal. It is in short, the personal- growth function.

Appraisal and evaluation. Our mindfulness not only needs to facilitate our understanding of ourselves, but also make sense out of the environment in which we live. Social and technological change, seem to be inevitable but little else can be assured. As a necessary first step to adaptation we need to be evaluating the situations confronting us and which we move through going forward in our daily lives.

Decision making. At every moment we come to a choice point in which we need to determine which way to go. The best decisions will be informed by circumstances and will be rational and logical. We want to go in the direction of utility or workability and harmoniousness or fittingness. In any case, we make our fate by the decisions we take (Sartre, as quoted by Jones, 2012).

Tuning in-to who we are. An important idea, but not new. While I associate the notion with the psychology of personal growth and positive mental health, tuning-in has a long lineage. Here are just a few quotes:

Know Thyself. *Socrates*

It is wisdom to know others; It is enlightenment to know one's self. *Lao-Tzu*

Observe all men; thyself most. *Benjamin Franklin*

Man's main task in life is to give birth to himself. *Erich Fromm*

Understanding ourselves in the natural and the social setting in which we live can pay important dividends. It provides a means for seeing ourselves and the forces that impinge upon us. This kind of self-knowledge has been called dynamic self-understanding (Carkhuff and Berenson, 1967). So, how did we get to where we now find ourselves? Did we follow family tradition, depart from that tradition or adopt a new model of who we want to be? We want to understand our history in relation to our present and be sure that this understanding informs our course and trajectory toward the future.

Accepting and coming to terms with ourselves. As we understand who we are, we need to be able to accept ourselves. Life as a unique individual is not always easy and it will be important to us to accept and value who we are and how we got to be who we are, or to resolve to make changes. (cf. Demo, 1992)

Finding our path to peace and harmony. Grit is required to find peace and harmony but there is no magic to invoke to get it. It derives from emotional self-management and resource management, including energy and vitality management. In

Chapter 18 : Fearless Being and Becoming?

interpersonal situations, grit emerges as much out of what we don't say or do as it is out of what we actually say or do.

There might concern that, while this is a simple model, putting it into practice would be challenging. To the contrary, most of us do all of these things all the time, as a matter of routine. When we see it written out in the conceptual model, it may start to look mystifying and intimidating, but I think we just do it quite automatically. For example, as kids we think about what we want to do when we grow up, assisted by the adults around us who seem to relentlessly ask this question. As adults we look around to see what other people are doing in their lives and identify what might work for us. Without much fanfare, we begin identifying the pieces necessary to start the required tasks and move forward in a stepwise fashion. In short, I am saying that we already do this, but with increased awareness we can make it work even better.

We have looked at two models of how we function in our daily lives and over our lifespan. These models are to help us identify our goals and possible paths. As we get more comfortable in our own skin and with the natural world around us, we can be increasingly comfortable with the uncertainties and stresses of our lives.

I have found it informative to reflect on, "An Eschatological Laundry List," offered by Sheldon Kopp (1974). In theology, the word "eschatology" has to do with the study of events that occur at the end of the sequence and in particular refer to the end of the world, or the climax of history, as in the:

final event in the divine plan;
end of the world;
gift of eternal life at the eschaton. (cf. xforddictionaries.com)

This list appears in an appendix of Dr. Kopp's book and it's not clear just how it was intended. In my view, it provides a kind of "let go and make the best of our world" perspective, consistent with both the existentialists and the Buddhists. See what you think.

An Eschatological Laundry List

This is it.

There are no hidden meanings.

You can't get there from here, and besides there is no place to go.

Nothing lasts!

We can't have anything unless we let go of it.

There is no particular reason why you lost out on some things.

We have the responsibility to do our best nonetheless.

It's a random universe to which we bring meaning.

We really don't control anything.

Everyone is, in their own way, vulnerable.

If you have a hero, look again; you have diminished yourself in some way.

Everyone lies, cheats, pretends. (yes, you too, and most certainly myself.)

All evil is potentially vitality in need of transformation.

Progress is an illusion.

Evil can be displaced but never eradicated, as all solutions breed new problems.

Yet it is necessary to keep struggling toward solution.

Each of us is ultimately alone.

The most important things each person does for themselves.

Love is not enough, but it sure helps.

Chapter 18 : Fearless Being and Becoming?

How strange, that so often, it all seems worth it.

It is most important to run out of scapegoats.

We must learn the power of living with our helplessness.

The only victory lies in surrender to oneself.

All of the significant battles are waged within the self.

We are free to do whatever we like. We need only face the consequences.

What do we know for sure...anyway?

Learn to forgive yourself, again and again and again and again.

> Excerpted and edited from:
> http://peterfox.com.au/manifesto_kopp.html. For the sake of economy I have excerpted down to 27. Dr. Kopp offered a total of 43 items.

In case you're interested in doing a toe test of the Buddhist tradition, there is a Buddhist inspired movie that provides an easy opportunity to get a sense of what they are saying. *Peaceful Warrior* (2006) is the story of an aspiring gymnast who wants to compete in the Olympics. The promotional material describes it as, "Like Rocky for the Soul," and also "A Movie That Changes Lives." I find it to be a charming and a "feel good piece" that is consistent with the Buddhist world view.

Q & A

This book sure seems to have lists. Do I need to memorize all the lists in order to make this thing work?

In this chapter the lists are part of a thought exercise and a conceptual model about how we routinely function in the world. My goal here is to develop a line of thinking, a logic that is clearly understandable and therefor challengeable by readers. It would surely be worthwhile to understand how Mindfulness, Being, Becoming,

Appraisal, Decision-Making, Tuning In, Accepting, and Peace might be reasonable goals in our lives.

This "Laundry List" from psychologist Sheldon Kopp looks like bad news. Items like:
This if it
We are already dying...
Nothing lasts
It's a random universe...
Learn to forgive yourself, again and again and again and again have about as much brightness and cheer as the Buddhists or existentialists.

You got it! As noted in the preparation for our reflecting on the "List," it is quite consistent with both of the Buddhist and the existentialists. I continued to believe that these folks are sharing something very important to us. We can not only reduce the pain in our lives but we can increase our joy as we come to terms with the insights offered by the Buddhists, the existentialists, and the "Laundry List" offered by Dr. Kopp.

Chapter 19
Can't I Just Have What I Want?
Tolerance and Craving

Overview

We look at how we relate to one another in a pluralistic society, revisit deficiency motivation, and consider how people may acquire a worldview.

Tolerance?

We all have needs and wants. Needs come in many sizes, beginning with the safety-security and moving toward self-actualization and maximizing our potential. Wants are a bit more expansive, but they often come with a price tag attached. The question of satisfying individual needs at the expense of our neighbors or the larger community emerges frequently. As we learned in grade school, we need to avoid interfering with the rights of others. World history includes an array of incidents of disregarding or interfering with the rights of others. Wars of aggression or campaigns of extermination come to mind. However, there are many less blatant, but still damaging intrusions, often on minorities.

The spectacle of religious persecution is quite scary. There is little doubt harassment continues:

Throughout centuries of history, persecution for religious belief has existed in every age and every nation. It is at the root of many conflicts throughout the world, even today. The interesting thing about religious oppression is, it rarely arises from irreligion, but rather from one religion or religious sect persecuting the beliefs of those who differ from them. (Religious oppression . . ., 2013)

The First Amendment to the US Constitution states in part, "Congress shall make no law respecting an establishment of religion, or prohibiting the free exercise thereof . . . ." This is, of course, the fundamental basis for freedom of religion in the US. I also take it as a personal admonition that, if there is to be anything sacred in my world, it must be the religious views, practices and sensitivities of others. I take the First Amendment to admonish me, personally, not to judge the religion of anyone else. As far as I am concerned, religion, spirituality, faith, mysticism, agnosticism or atheism are the personal and sacrosanct choices of individuals. For me, there remains great importance to not only honor the styles and sentiments of those around me, but also to celebrate them as yet another instance of the expansive value of diversity.

This book includes text and tables making comparisons of various worldviews. From time to time I have pointed out that such comparisons are based on a functional analysis. The emphasis here is to consider how a particular worldview will function for a person who adopts it in a real life situation. I don't presume to judge religion and spirituality, Eastern cultural traditions juxtaposed to Western cultural traditions, etc., only to develop the notion of where the ideas might take us in our lives.

Whatever our worldview, there are usually counterparts, opposite numbers and contrary views bringing the challenge for us of just what is reasonable to believe. Our world presents us with an enormous variety of differences in climate, geographic, social, cultural, racial and world views. It is a bounty to behold. So, how do

Chapter 19 : Can't I Just Have What I Want?

we accommodate, tolerate, or otherwise cope with these substantive and stylistic differences among us? What if the differences are in our own family? It does not seem to me to be any easier to be a kid than a parent. Both kids and parents are engaged in their roles in the relationship for the first time and have to learn by doing. A quote from social worker, family therapist and author, Virginia Satir renders it this way:

> Feelings of worth can flourish only in an atmosphere where individual differences are appreciated, mistakes are tolerated, communication is open, and rules are flexible - the kind of atmosphere that is found in a nurturing family.

We are often willing to make exceptions or special allowances for family. But, what about other differences like regional, national origin, religious, political, social class, economic interest, ethnic or racial? Are these "others" to be accepted, trusted, allowed to marry our brothers, sisters or sons and daughters? Diversity can empower us in many ways:

How can you govern a country which has 246 varieties of cheese? *Charles de Gaulle*

Travel is fatal to prejudice, bigotry, and narrow-mindedness, and many of our people need it sorely on these accounts. Broad, wholesome, charitable views of men and things cannot be acquired by vegetating in one little corner of the earth all one's lifetime *Mark Twain*

Christian, Jew, Muslim, shaman, Zoroastrian, stone, ground, mountain, river, each has a secret way of being with the mystery, unique and not to be judged. *Rumi*

It is never too late to give up your prejudices. *Henry David Thoreau*
Strength lies in differences, not in similarities. *Stephen R. Covey*

In my view, we need to be able to, not only to tolerate our differences of world view and belief, and all the rest, but also to celebrate them. While I agree with Mark Twain about acquiring wholesome views of others, travel makes for an expensive adventure. We need to be able to experience different life styles and world views in a living embodiment in our every-day world. How else can we figure out who we are, ourselves?

We have been talking about the benefits and advantages of diversity in our midst. But what happens if we fail to recognize our commonalities and therefore cannot appreciate or celebrate our differences? Could anything go wrong for our society or ourselves? Martin Niemöller (US Holocaust Museum, 2013) put his view in poetic form. He was a prominent Protestant pastor who emerged as an outspoken public foe of Adolf Hitler and spent the last seven years of Nazi rule in concentration camps:

> First they came for the Socialists, and I did not speak out--
> Because I was not a Socialist.
> Then they came for the Trade Unionists, and I did not speak out--
> Because I was not a Trade Unionist.
> Then they came for the Jews, and I did not speak out--
> Because I was not a Jew.
> Then they came for me—
> And there was no one left to speak for me.
> *Martin Niemöller*

I argue there are considerable personal and social advantages to celebrating our differences. What is more, there is potentially catastrophic disadvantages to failing to connect to others, or failure to take exception to discrimination against others, much less imprisonment or worse, for our fellow human beings.

Chapter 19 : Can't I Just Have What I Want?

Deficiency and Cravings

In Chapter 2, we looked briefly at the notion of the behavioral trap. We discussed the downward spiral of anxiety, angst and craving. At that time we had identified some stressors and negative emotional states that might bring us to a place in which we were in very severe need of recovery and positive growth. I argue that rather than allowing ourselves to be motivated by negative, deficiency needs, we might want to regain our footing and move toward achieving our positive, growth needs. But, what is this behavioral trap?

The notion of the behavioral trap was first offered by Baer and Wolf (1970) to describe how natural contingencies of reinforcement (reward) operate to promote and maintain behavior changes. The essence of a trap is that only a relatively simple response is necessary to enter the trap. But once in it, the trap it is difficult to exit. Consider the common mouse trap. All that is needed is a response triggered by the aroma of the bait. In our circumstances, once we begin focusing on negative emotional states and negative (dysfunctional) behaviors, escape is dramatically more difficult. Caught in the prongs of the trap, we might very well spiral down, as though propelled by a fluted anchor, to the sea bed. We need to learn to recognize traps in advance, identify our own feelings and behavior patterns, and take precautions to head off our own self-entrapping behavior. Action is best taken early in a behavioral sequence. For example, anyone with any hint of a drinking problem had better avoid stopping at the local bar, just for the sandwiches.

Behaviors occur in sequences or chains of events in which one leads to the next. Each event becomes a trigger for the next action in the sequence. At work, try stopping at the water cooler or the break room and not talking to colleagues who show up for relief from the pressures of the day, like you. The classic line from the old western movies, "Head 'em off at the pass," can be applied here. We want to intervene in sequences of dysfunctional behavior early, ASAP. For example, if there is any problem with smoking too many cigarettes, try spending more time in the local swimming pool. "Head 'em off at the pass!" might be a useful self-prompt to avoid problem behavior.

There might be some concern that it is hard to avoid paying attention to the negative and when we know our behavior is out of bounds and we are sinking? We need to be focusing on the positive as much as we can. Ordinary personal exercises include identifying the useful personal skills that we bring to interpersonal situations and problem-solving situations. There may be a lot of things we do which don't work very well for us; it will be important to focus on the things that we do which are positive and helpful for us. There is a helpful computer game called, "Mind Habits Trainer," (Baldwin, 2012) which is useful in training up this behavior. The caution is, this is just a computer game cartoon-like graphics developed by social psychologists to help us focus on the positive and help with relaxation. It is not any sort of "shoot 'em-up-game" to be used on a sophisticated gaming console. Mind Habits Trainer uses a variety of strategies to help us focus on the positive. The easiest one to understand is, "click on the smiling face." While it looks simple at first, it quickly moves along to higher complexity from two faces to four and eight, as well as with shorter time allowances to achieve the goal required to reach the next level. But this is just one of multiple challenging visual discrimination tasks. The research findings indicate positive outcomes (Dandeneau, Baldwin, Baccus, Sakellaropoulo & Pruessner, 2007).

If we don't stay focused on the positive, could we get caught in tension, low mood and longing for what we do not have? Does the mass-media and advertising invite us to expect more goodies than we can possibly enjoy, much less afford? Could life as a consumer be more stressful than the good life we are invited to pursue is actually beneficial? Does social-media encourage us to make negative comparisons of our situation to that of others? Is malaise just our era, or has it always been challenging to keep a perspective on our lives, and our place in society and the larger scheme of things? I think there

Chapter 19 : Can't I Just Have What I Want?

are probably many more issues, but we know what we are up against. We also know that the technical face on the devices and gadgets may be new, but the problem is as old as time.

Wishes, wants, longings, yearnings and cravings remain powerful mechanisms of dissatisfaction. We live in an era in which independent-mindedness may even be more important than social connectedness. We need to be able to identify who we are and define ourselves against a strong tide of social homogenization.

How can we find true happiness? Opinions differ widely, and some are really fun.

It's pretty hard to tell what does bring happiness. Poverty and wealth have both failed. *Frank McKinney*

Contentment is natural wealth, luxury is artificial poverty. *Socrates*
Do not spoil what you have by desiring what you have not.
Ann Brashares

There are two things to aim at in life: first, to get what you want; and after that, to enjoy it. Only the wisest of mankind achieve the second. *Logan Pearsall Smith*

Cheerfulness is what greases the axles of the world. Don't go through life creaking. *H.W. Byles*

If you want others to be happy, practice compassion. If you want to be happy, practice compassion. *Dalai Lama*

Life Goals and Views

The meaning of life is one of the eternal questions and is perhaps even more basic than the meaning of freedom or justice. Each culture and era seem to redefine it in their own way, but the question seems never to be settled. For the sake of discussion only, here is a short list of common goals that are products of different world views:

> Realize one's potential and ideals
> Do the right thing
> Know God
> Find oneself
> Enjoy the act of living
> Know and master the world
> Assert that life has no meaning

In my view they have little overlap and seem to be talking about very different views or perceptions of the world.

How could it be that there are so many different views of the world? Our life experiences provide us with different viewpoints as a result of issues like setting, social history, circumstance, occupation, skill level, transactional role (buyer or seller), social status, incumbent or insurgent, conservative or liberal, and many more. While it is just a single thread in a vast tapestry, Albert Ellis (Ellis & Dryden, 2007) has offered the A, B, C paradigm to explain how particular beliefs can affect our thoughts and behavior:

A, B, C Paradigm / Model:

> A. Something happens.
> B. You have a belief about the situation.
> C. You have an emotional reaction to the belief.
> Example:
> A. Your supervisor falsely accuses you of taking money from her purse and threatens to
>> fire you.
>
> B. You believe, "She has no right to accuse me. She's a witch!"
> C. You feel angry.
>
> Explanation:
> If you had held a different belief, your emotional response

Chapter 19 : Can't I Just Have What I Want?

would have been different:

At A, your supervisor falsely accuses you of taking money from her purse and threatens to fire you. At B, you believe, "I must not lose my job. That would be unbearable."

At C, you feel anxious.

The ABC model shows that A does not cause C. It is B that causes C.

While there are likely to be many other mechanisms for generating our own viewpoint the A, B, C paradigm gets us off on the right foot in our thinking about the process.

Q & A

What is this stuff about, "I take the First Amendment to admonish me, personally, not to judge the religion of anyone else." Wouldn't you want to cut yourself a little slack?

As a kid in school I regarded the founding documents of the US to be compelling and expansive. The Bill of Rights and the enforcement of it by the Supreme Court continue to inspire me. It is my hope that, not only will the government continue to work for the people, but also that we have some hope of protection when government fails, in the form of Court decision.

We have not heard your view of the meaning of life. Are you going to tell?

It is still one of those eternal questions to which I can claim no special expertise. I am a psychologist and a seeker on my path. What I can offer is that I have long held the view that meaning is inherent in life and cannot be separated from it. Perhaps the following quotation frames this more succinctly:

> I was interested in finding a quotation that gets right at the issue: "Life has no meaning. Each of us has meaning and we bring it to life. It is a waste to be asking the question when

you are the answer." *Joseph Campbell*

Chapter 20
Are We Unstoppable Now?
Real Limitations

Overview

We look at the question of validity, or the accuracy of the model. It's not sufficient to just ask for testimonials. The question is whether these ideas really work in the natural world. We need objective verification.

Quotations

The man with insight enough to admit his limitations comes nearest to perfection. *Goethe*

The greatest intelligence is precisely the one that suffers most from its own limitations. *Andre Gide*

We must learn our limits. We are all something, but none of us are everything. *Pascal*

Any Other Explanation?

In multiple chapters we have looked at the mechanisms by which various components of the model may actually work. We talked about the breath control relaxation exercise and its possible relationship to the diving response as well as meditation itself and how it might relate to a treatment called systematic desensitization of phobia. But there is the lingering question; are these comparisons and or metaphors really accurate? For the writer of such notions the simple solution is to say, "Why not?" That is, why wouldn't it work? The problem of course is that this gets things backwards. The explanations provided in the relaxation and meditation chapters describe how they might work but there is the lingering question of whether the full model actually does what it says it does.

While it seems to be a bit far-fetched to me, some might argue that positive outcomes described in previous chapters are the result of the placebo effect. Simply put, the sugar pill did it. It is that it is not unreasonable to consider this possibility (c.f. placebo-effect, 2014). The notion is, unintended parts of a treatment intervention may turn out to quite powerful unintended effects. Proper consideration needs to be given to both intended and unintended effects of the treatment (self-help) process.

A related phenomenon is known as Hawthorne effect, named for the psychologist who first uncovered it. While completing a series of studies about the effect of working conditions on the quality of production, he found that production improved when improvements were made to lighting conditions in a factory setting. Not content with these encouraging findings, Hawthorne further manipulated the environment to degrade working conditions. Production got better yet again. The explanation given is, workers on the shop floor respond positively to environmental changes perceived to be positive, whether they are or not (c.f. Hawthorne effect, 2008).

A loosely related phenomenon also needs to be mentioned. Hypnosis has long caught the attention of the general public. It seems to present the attractions of being simple, direct, and powerful, while perhaps at the same time being somehow illegitimate. In professional circles it is not without controversy. There are those who argue that real hypnosis can be achieved only by "hypnotic induction" (c.f. Hilgard, 1965) and there are naysayers who argue anything that can be produced by hypnotic induction can be

Chapter 20 : Are We Unstoppable Now?

produced with direct instructions (c.f. Barber, 1969). The notion of self-hypnosis applied to any current situation would simply assert that people are doing something that "changes their mental state" and such a change is the true mechanism for the positive changes that are reported when people practice relaxation or meditation exercises.

Just to sharpen the problem a little, do the positive's before relaxation and meditation come from these exercises or from some incidental part of the procedure used? For me, the notion of self-hypnosis doesn't seem to add anything to the practices described here. Furthermore the notions of hypnotic induction versus direct instruction are so different that it does not seem to me that making such an argument would not be credible. The enormous difference in worldviews of the two major sides who argue for the use of hypnosis seem to be irreconcilable at this time and, until there's some clarity about how it actually works, I surely would not want to be using it as an explanatory concept.

Research Is Needed

I have provided text citations and a reference list so that readers might have the opportunity to track the development of my line of argument. There are a few new ideas and they simply have not been tested. I am a psychologist of long experience and great enthusiasm. For me, that argues even more strongly for empirical validation of the ideas offered. Isn't that too high a standard, you might ask? Not at all. In the long run empirical studies will be required to see if we are on the right track, or where tune-up is needed.

Three kinds of studies would be easy to envision:

Effectiveness of breath control relaxation and the modified model of meditation.

Individual outcomes of research subjects who apply this model or some sham treatment.

Global measures of mental health outcomes.

Q & A

Who would do the research? Is it by invitation only?
New ideas, like applying a modified meditation procedure to sort out and resolve life / death concerns, would be a tempting target (I hope) for psychologists or others interested in how behavior change works.

Is it okay to try this stuff before the research is completed?
Sure. We all have ideas, hunches, or insights that point us in new directions in our daily chores or big projects. Fire when ready.

Chapter 21
From Angst to Acceptance?
A View from the Path

Overview

As we move toward a close, we look at the implications of being on our path, including risks, and what the path might and might not provide.

Quotations

Life is a journey, not a destination. *Ralph Waldo Emerson*

And if there were a God, I think it very unlikely that He would have such an uneasy vanity as to be offended by those who doubt His existence. *Bertrand Russell*

There are only two tragedies in life: one is not getting what one wants, and the other is getting it. *Oscar Wilde*

You only lose what you cling to. *Buddha*

I have learned to seek my happiness by limiting my desires, rather than in attempting to satisfy them. *John Stuart Mill*

Life is problems. Living is solving problems. *Raymond E. Feist*

I have no money, no resources, no hopes. I am the happiest man alive. *Henry Miller*

On Our Path

I am a seeker, like you. I am on my path and finding my way. It doesn't matter whether one of us is ahead or behind. We are both on our paths, and chances are we are in about the right place for each of us. With this book we have a chart to help us navigate our course. While this is a life-long quest, we can follow it at home or away and in our spare time.

Once we are on our path, is it possible to make mistakes? I can assure you I make many of them every day. We don't get to be Wonder Woman or Superman just by finding our path. The path is simply a reality-based way of coping with some of the problems we face in everyday life and in the longer sweep of our lives toward its conclusion. The path is not based on wishes, hopes, fantasy, magic, or sleight-of-hand. It does not offer any guarantees and in itself does not constitute an attainment. It's simply an avenue, some blaze marks to indicate a likely trail. I have tried to offer an understandable logic of how the pieces go together, so that anyone can test it out and challenge my conclusions. There is no leap of faith (Kierkegaard, (1844 / 1980) required here. To the contrary, we need to bring our experience, skepticism, logic and problem solving skills to this journey.

The journey of life is universal, but we all need to understand the problems we face in our unique situation. Sometimes we find ourselves going up blind alleys with solutions that do not adequately address our problems. No matter what efforts we make, the big question is whether we are getting the job done. If not, we need to make course changes.

By contrast, during the 1960's and for many years, the American humorist Gene Shepherd (cf. *In God We Trust, All Others Pay Cash*, 1966) talked in jest on his New York-based radio program about the idea of a "fulfillment pill." The notion is, if you're not

Chapter 21 : From Angst to Acceptance

feeling up to par, just take a pill and it will satisfy your life needs. He had his finger on the pulse of the American excess use of pharmaceuticals and illegal drugs. This book is hardly talking about instant fulfillment, but rather global understandings, a conceptual model, the disappointments and realities of the human experience and the use of available methods to address life's challenges.

Having developed our own relaxation and meditation skills, we just might be able to adopt a strategy from the experiential psychotherapists (cf. Gendlin, 1998). They recommend, if there is something bothering us, we ask ourselves an ordinary question like, "What is it?" They point out, if we can be sufficiently still, sometimes we may get an answer. Since we are on our path, we have tools available to resolve problems. However, as we already know, it will take emotional and intellectual work to stay on the path.

Prudent Risk

In starting on our path, are we taking unnecessary risk? Are there unintended consequences to doing what we have set ourselves to do? We need to be able to consider the implications of the path. Religious angst and the worry, fear, and anxiety that go with it may be painful and even torturous. Regardless of our spiritual, religious or theological background, I would guess we've all had a taste of the experience. We need to focus on moving toward our positive goals of contentment with the recognition of what is do-able in our lives.

In our natural world there are things that go together organically and logically just the way we find them. For example, apples and cherries grow well in Michigan. There are also things that are not naturally occurring together and do not go together logically. For example,

Florida worm lizards do well in Florida, not very well in the temperatures of Michigan. That is, one event necessarily excludes the other. In this case, we are seekers and hence we cannot be gurus. We have an opportunity before us, but it does not constitute an achievement, since we have yet to follow it through to a conclusion.

The path will allow us to release some of our longings and cravings and, hence, they will have less impact on our lives. We make it a point to move toward what works for us in our lives, rather than merely fleeing from what doesn't. Since we acknowledge only a natural world, we cannot lose a faith, or soul, which are inconsistent with the natural world. Similarly we can't be an infidel, because we do not deny the existence of an external deity that we never believed in. The SBNG

world view does not endorse faith, religiosity or theology that presumes an external, supernatural God. Because we each decide what works best for us, there is no creedal requirement for which a leap of faith might be needed. Since there is no priesthood, religious expert, or ultimate authority, there cannot be any heresy, excommunication or inquisition.

The table below provides a comparison of the polar extremes of what the path is likely to provide and not likely to provide. All such comparisons are simplifications and there are always exceptions

Table 21.1 What Following Our Path Can and Can't Provide

Provides	Does not Provide
Seeker	Guru
Opportunity	Achievement
Letting go	Craving, grasping, clutching, clinging, angst
Moving forward, going toward	Fleeing from
Natural world	Lose faith or soul, infidel
SPNG	Religion, Theology, Faith
Test, try-out, decide	Leap of faith
No priesthood, hierarchy or ultimate authority	Heresy, excommunication, inquisition

Chapter 21 : From Angst to Acceptance

Acceptance

While we may have difficulty embracing the idea of the end of our lives, it will be important to accept it. Still, acceptance is not without some obstacles. As I turn it over in my mind, I'm aware of a sense experience of the world with eyes, ears, nose, fingers and toes and anything that hurts. This experience seems entirely ordinary and has been predictable during the course of my life. There is also another dimension of memory, reflection and contemplation that goes with our
perceptions and seems to be organic to our life experience. The ending, lapsing or termination of these experiences seems hard to imagine.

As I turn over such thoughts, it comes through that I seem to you experience some sort of entitlement to life. As if somehow life everlasting is owed to me. It is true that I can remember no state other than life. Could I be so accustomed to life that I can imagine no other state? Is it that I have come to see eternal life as a birth right, taking life for granted? Needless to say these issues are emotional rather than logical or empirical. I want, what I want and it is continued life, as I would like to have lived it. Am I the only one who just can't get it? Not to worry, I think these are universal feelings.

As we discussed in Chapter 7, there are powerful natural forces all around us.

The interactions of these forces set the rules of operation for our world and we are clearly subordinate to them. We are not in charge here, but rather privileged to live a life under the auspices of a cosmos with many, as yet, undiscovered properties and mechanisms. We are part of the natural world around us in which the progression of birth to death is quite visible in the plants and animals with which we share this world. We might have grandparents whom we never met and there are certainly ancient forbearers with whom we may not have experienced any connection, but if it were not for them we would not be here. We are at the leading edge of a chain of life.

Perhaps an analogy is the social and political worlds in which we live. It's not going to work very well to reject our families, neighbors, school officials and work supervisors, since we live in an interconnected system of which we are only a part. It's tempting to think that we can only acquiesce, give our assent, and accede to the superior powers around us. But this would miss the point that we live in an ecology, a massive cosmic system, in which we have the privilege of briefly participating. As we noted early on in this discussion we are temporary here. Perhaps the more general principle is that this larger world, in which we dwell, if we work hard, will allow us to garner the resources to live rewarding lives of awakening, peace and harmony.

Source of Inspiration

Just like other seekers, as I researched this book I located many earlier works from a variety of long-standing traditions. I found the Buddhists to be the most helpful to me. As I look over the various wisdom traditions, what came through clearly to me was the need for a methodology. The question is, "What should we *do* to follow the path?" The path to peace and harmony is not only about wisdom, it is also about *practice*. The Buddhists, and many others, have meditation practices that can best be understood as a "technology," in the modern sense. As discussed in Chapter 13, while the Buddhists have different goals, their technology is easily adapted to our needs. Used in combination with relaxation training skills from psychology, we have been able to adapt off-the-shelf technologies to our needs.

Ready, Steady, Go

Having developed our own relaxation and meditation skills, it might be interesting to consider greater involvement with one of the meditative traditions. Perhaps we might consider becoming Buddhist or at least becoming more aware of the Buddhist tradition. The

Chapter 21 : From Angst to Acceptance

Buddhists, or any of the other contemplative traditions, would welcome neophytes into a beginning exploration. Web searches can quickly identify how to get in touch with people to get started in any of the meditative traditions. There is a great variety of information on the web regarding entering one of these traditions. I found sites that offer the possibility of becoming a Buddhist by reciting a few chants, after which I would officially be a Buddhist. I was struck that other Buddhist sites urged a deliberative approach to making such a substantial commitment and which specifically counseled the importance of understanding the tradition before making any extravagant statements about our intentions or making any personal commitments. I would think there is plenty of time to consider what might be our best choices.

But, aren't we in a battle against time to find our path? What if we don't find our path before we die? Will we be in some kind of trouble? No trouble. Finding our path is really about living, not about dying. The sooner we find our own path, whatever its nature, the sooner we can move toward a life of peace and harmony.

I have made my choice to follow the path outlined in this book since it obviously fits me. It does represent a substantial formalization of what I have been thinking and doing over the years and fits me well. Still, for each of us there are decisions to make every day about our path. Are we feeling: better, worse or about the same? Should we buy more, sell what we have or hold on to it? We looked at an approach to the challenge of living in an uncertain world in Chapter 6 in the form of questions offered in *Buddhism Without Beliefs:*

> Since death alone is certain and the time of death uncertain, what should I do? (Batchelor, 1997, p 32)

Only our own personal answers to this question will be relevant here. We might want to make plans for what we know we want to do.

Perhaps The Buddha said it best:

No one saves us but ourselves.
No one can and no one may.
We ourselves must walk the path.

Mini-Glossary

Because of the specialized vocabulary used in discussing and understanding this material, and it seemed to be important to provide a mini-glossary to help us out a bit. The definitions come from common dictionary and encyclopedia sources (See below) and the items are arranged in alphabetical order. Where there are multiple meanings, only the application closest to book our supply. Note that some writers may go back to older, common definitions or use new personal definitions for their particular discussion.

Agnostic- A person who holds the view that any ultimate reality (as God) is unknown and probably unknowable; broadly one who is not committed to believing in either the existence or the nonexistence of God or a god.

Atheist- One who believes that there is no deity.

Creed- A brief authoritative formula of religious belief.

Deity- Capitalized: God, Supreme Being.

Deism- A movement or system of thought advocating natural religion, emphasizing morality, and in the 18th century denying the interference of the Creator with the laws of the universe

Devout- Devoted to religion or to religious duties or exercises.

Faith- Belief and trust in and loyalty to God. 2. Belief in the traditional doctrines of a religion. Firm belief in something for which there is no proof. 3. Complete trust.

God- Capitalized: The supreme or ultimate reality: as The Being perfect in power, wisdom, and goodness who is worshipped as.

Idolatry- The worship of a physical object as a god.

Magic- The use of means (as charms or spells) believed to have supernatural power over natural forces

Meditation- The act or process of spending time in quiet thought: the act or process of meditating

Myth- Usually traditional story of ostensibly historical events that serves to unfold part of the world view of a people or explain a practice, belief, or natural phenomenon.

Mysticism- A religious practice based on the belief that knowledge of spiritual truth can be gained by praying or thinking deeply.

Phenomenology- Phenomenology is the study of structures of consciousness as experienced from the first-person point of view. The central structure of an experience is its intentionality, its being directed toward something, as it is an experience of or about some object. An experience is directed toward an object by virtue of its content or meaning (which represents the object) together with appropriate enabling conditions.

http://plato.stanford.edu/entries/phenomenology/

Phenomenological- Of or relating to phenomenology

Prayer- To make a request in a humble manner. To address God or a god with adoration, confession, supplication, or thanksgiving

Quasi (Prefix)- Having some resemblance usually by possession of certain attributes a quasi-corporation

Religion- Relating to or manifesting faithful devotion to an acknowledged ultimate reality

Religious- Relating to or manifesting faithful devotion to an acknowledged ultimate reality or deity <a religious person> <religious attitudes>

Religiosity- 1. The quality of being religious; piety; devoutness. 2. Affected or excessive devotion to religion. (http://dictionary.reference.com/browse/religiosity)

Religious experience- Religious experiences can be characterized

Mini-Glossary

generally as experiences that seem to the person having them to be of some objective reality and to have some religious import. That reality can be an individual, a state of affairs, a fact, or even an absence, depending on the religious tradition the experience is a part of. A wide variety of kinds of experience fall under the general rubric of religious experience. The concept is vague, and the multiplicity of kinds of experiences that fall under it makes it difficult to capture in any general account. (http://plato.stanford.edu/entries/religious-experience/)

Ritual- Of or relating to rites or a ritual. Ceremonial <a ritual dance. According to religious law; ritual purity.

Spirituality- Of, relating to, consisting of, or affecting the spirit: incorporeal

Supernatural- Of or relating to an order of existence beyond the visible observable universe; especially: of or relating to God or a god, demigod, spirit, or devil

Superstition- A belief or practice resulting from ignorance, fear of the unknown, trust in magic or chance, or a false conception of causation

Theism- Belief in the existence of a god or gods, specifically of a creator who intervenes in the universe: there are many different forms of theism. Compare with deism.

(http://oxforddictionaries.com/definition/english/theism)

Theology- 1. The study of religious faith, practice, and experience; especially the study of God and of God's relation to the world

Worship- Reverence offered a divine being or supernatural power; also : an act of expressing such reverence. A form of religious practice with its creed and ritual

Source: http://www.merriam-webster.com/dictionary, except as noted.

Life, Death and Spirituality

References

ARIS. (2008). URL: http://www.gc.cuny.edu/Faculty/GC-Faculty-Activities/ARIS--American-Religious-Identification-Survey/Key-findings

A Basic Buddhism Guide: 5 Minute Introduction. Retrieved March 19, 2012 from: http://www.buddhanet.net/e-learning/5minbud.htm

A Basic Buddhism Guide: Introduction to Buddhism. (2012) Retrieved April 25,2012 from: http://www.buddhanet.net/e-learning/intro_bud.htm.

Adams, M. M. & Adams, R. M. (Eds.). (1991). *The problem of evil.* New York: Oxford University Press.

Anwar, Y. (2013) Americans and religion increasingly parting ways, new survey shows. Retrieved Sept. 18, 2013 from http://newscenter.berkeley.edu/2013/03/12/non-believers/

Adams, S. (2001). *God's debris: A thought experiment.* Kansas City: Andrews McMeel.

Allport, G.W. (1955). Becoming: Basic considerations for a psychology of personality. New Haven: Yale University Press.

Barawoski, J. (1974). *The Ascent of Man.* (DVD, Time/Life-BBC). New York: Ambrose Video Publishing.

Batchelor, S. (1997) *Buddhism without Beliefs: A Contemporary Guide to Awakening.* New York: Riverhead Books.

Baldwin, M. W. (2012) Mindhabits: Games for a positive outlook. Amazon Digital Services. ASIN: B0070OZJBO.

Baer, D. M., & Wolf, M. M. (1970). The entry into natural communities of reinforcement. In R. Ulrich, T. Stachnick, & J. Mabry (Eds.) Control of human behavior (pp. 319-324).Glenview, IL: Scott Foresman.

Barber, T.X., (1969) Hypnosis: A Scientific Approach, N.Y.: Van Nostrand Reinhold.

Berkobin, Fred (1966 f) Personal Communication.

Bibikova, A. & Kotelnikov, V. (2013) East versus west: Philosophy, cultural values and mindset. Retrieved May 1, 2013 from: 1000ventures.com/ business_guide/crosscuttings/cultures_east-west-philosophy.html

Basics of Buddhism (2012) Retrieved June 29, 2012 from: http://www. letusreason.org/Buddh1.htm

Bierce, A. (1993) *The devil's dictionary.* Mineola, New York:: Dover.

Branowski, Jacob. (1974). *The Ascent of Man.* Boston: Little, Brown.

Breathology (2012). The mammalian diving reflex. Retrieved 7-2-2012 from /services/articles/freediving/the-mammalian-diving-reflex

Cahn, R. & John, P. Meditation states and traits: EEG, ERP, and neuroimaging studies. (2006, March). Psychological Bulletin 132 (2): 180–211

Calvin, John (1536) Institutes of the Christian Religion. Retrieved July 10, 2013 from: http://academic. brooklyn.cuny.edu/history/dfg/amrl/calvin.htm

Carkhuff, R. & Berenson, B. (1967) Beyond counseling and therapy. New York: Holt, Rinehart andWinston.

Chambers, Chuen-Yee &, Allen, N. B. (2008) The impact of intensive mindfulness training on attentional control, cognitive style, and affect. Cognitive Therapy Research 32:303–322

Clark, D. A. & Beck, A. T. (2011) Cognitive therapy of anxiety disorders. New York: Guilford.

Cooley, C. H. (1902). *Human nature and the social order.* New York: Scribner's. CUNY Graduate Center (2001)

Comte-Sponville, A. (2007) The little book of atheist spirituality. NY, Penguin. Translation: Huston, N. ISBM: 978-0-14-311443-7

Conrad, A. & Roth, W. T. (2007) Muscle relaxation therapy for anxiety disorders: It works but how? Journal of Anxiety Disorders, 21 243–264.

Corr, C. A., Nabe C. M., & Corr, D.M. (2012) Death and dying, life and living. Beverly, MA, Wadsworth. Page 247 f

Crosthwaite , H. (2013) Looking like a God. Retrived June 26, 2013

References

from: http://www.grazian-archive.com/quantavolution/vol_12/ka_15.htm

Dandeneau, S. D., Baldwin, M. W., Baccus, J. R., Sakellaropoulo, M., & Pruessner, J. C. (2007). Cutting stress off at the pass: Reducing vigilance and responsiveness to social threat by manipulating attention. Journal of Personality and Social Psychology, 93, 651-666. See also: http://www.mindhabits.com

Dawkins, R. (1998) Unweaving the rainbow: science, delusion and appetite for wonder. New York: Mariner.

Dawkins, R. (2006). *The God delusion*. Boston: Houghton Mifflin.

Dawkins, R. (2009). *Greatest show on earth: The evidence for evolution* New York: Free Press.

DeGrazia, D. (2009) Death Stanford Encyclopedia of Philosophy.

Demo, David H. (1992). The self-concept over time: Research issues and directions. Annual Review of Sociology, 18, 303-326.

Dennett, D.C. (2007). *Breaking the spell: Religion as a natural phenomenon* New York: Penguin.

Earth from Space (2013). NOVA. Arlington, VA: PBS

Elliot, C. E. and Smith, L. L. (2003) Overcoming anxiety for dummies. New York: Wiley.

Ellis, A. & Dryden W. (2007) The practice of rational emotive behavior therapy. Oxford, England: Springer.

Fear-phobia, (2012) Retrieved March 27, 2014 from: http://www.statisticbrain.com/fear-phobia- statistics/

Epicurus Riddle: The Problem of evil (2012) Retrieved July 30, 2012 from: http://rkbentley.blogspot.com/2011/07/epicurus-riddle-problem-of-evil.html

Epistemology. (2012) In Stanford Encyclopedia of Philosophy. Retrieved July 6, 2012. http://plato.stanford.edu/entries/epistemology/

Fahs, Sophia Lyon (1993). It matters what we believe. (Responsive reading # 657) In: Unitarian Universalist Association *(1993) Singing the living tradition..* Boston: Beacon Press.

Fieser, James (2008) Great Issues in Philosophy, Retrieved 6-12-2013 from: http://www.utm.edu/staff/jfieser/class/120/1-meaning.htm

Fuller, R. C. (2001) Spiritual but not religious. New York: Oxford University Press.

Gendlin, E. T. (1998) Focusing-oriented psychotherapy: A manual of the experiential method. New York: Guilford.

Gallagher, B. (2012). *How to create your own religion in ten easy steps*! URL: http://www.apath.org/creating_religion.html

Gallup (2012). Americans' Spiritual Searches Turn Inward. URL: http://www.gallup.com /poll/7759/americans-spiritual-searches-turn-inward.aspx?version=print

Germ Theory (2012) Retrieved August 13, 2012 from: http://www.sciencemuseum.org/uk/broughttolife/techniques/germtheory.a spx

Gilbert, R. S. (2005*). Building your own theology: Vol. 2, Exploring.* Boston: Unitarian Universalist Association.

God in America (2010) Arlington, VA: PBS. Grief: Coping with reminders after a loss (2012) Retrieved Novembeer16, 2012 from: http://www.mayoclinic.com/health/grief/MH00036

Haidt, J. (2012). *The righteous mind: Why good people are divided by politics and religion.* New York: Pantheon.

Halevy, J. (2013) Does Transcendental Meditation Actually Work? Retrieved June 10, 2014 does-transcendental-meditat...

Harris, S. (2010). *The moral landscape.* New York: Free Press.

Harris, S. (2004). *The end of faith.* New York: Norton.

Hawking, S. (2010). *The grand design.* New York: Random House.

Hawthorne effect (2008). Retrieved September 29, 2014 from http://www.economist.com/node/12510632

Hill, N. (1937) *Think and grow rich.* Meriden, Connecticut: The Ralston Society.

Hilgard, E. R. (1965) Hypnotic susceptibility. Boston: Houghton, Mifflin, Harcourt.

References

Hitchens, C. (2007) *God is not great: How religion poisons everything.* Sydney. Allen & Unwin.

Hitchens, C. & Wilson, D. (2008). *Is Christianity Good for the World?* Moscow, ID: Canon Press.

Humanism (2012) Oxford Companion to Philosophy. Retrieved August 13, 2012 from: http://www.humanism.org.uk/humanism/

If wishes were horses… (2012) Retrieved October 4, 2012. http://en.wikipedia.org/wiki/If_wishes_were_horses,_beggars_would_ride

Inquisition (2012). Galileo Project. Retrieved June 20, 2012. http://galileo.rice.edu/chr/inquisition.html

Invention of Lying. (2009). Burbank, CA: Warner Brothers.

Jacobson, E. (1938). Progressive relaxation (2nd ed.). Chicago: University of Chicago Press.

Jensen, R. E. (1975). Cooperative relations between secondary teachers and students: Some behavioral strategies. Adolescence, 10, 469-482.

Jones, R. (2012) Philosophy and the proof of God's existence. Retrieved 1-5-2012 from: http://www.philosopher.org.uk/god.html

Jones, R. (2012). Existentialism. Retrieved June 6, 2012. http://www.philosopher.org.uk/existen.html

Kierkegaard, S. (1844 / 1980). *The Concept of Anxiety.* Reidar Thomte (Ed.) Princeton: Princeton University Press.

Koeller, D. W. (1996) Altamira Cave Paintings. Retrieved 7-24-2013 from: http://www. henagain.info/webchron/World/Altamira.html

Kopp, S. (1976). If you meet the Buddha on the road: Kill him. New York Lowe & Brydon (Printers) Ltd..

Kopp, S. (1991). *All God's children are lost, but only some can play the piano.* New York: Prentice-Hall.

LaFave, Sandra (2004). Comparing Eastern and Western Religions.Retrieved February 18, 2013 from: http://instruct.westvalleyedu/lafave/east_west.html

Landaw, J. , Bodian, S.and Buhnemann, G. (2011) Buddhism for dummies. (2nd Edition). Hoboken, NJ. Wiley.

Levy, D. M., Wobbrock, J.O., Kaszniak, A.K, Ostergren, M. (2012) The Effects of Mindfulness

Meditation Training on Multitasking in a High-Stress Information Environment. Front. Psychology, 3:116.doi:10.3389/fpsyg.2012.00116

Linehan, M. M. & Dimeff, L. (2001). Dialectical behavior therapy in a nutshell, The California Psychologist, 34, 10-13.

Lynch, D. (2014) Healing traumatic stress and raising performance in at-risk populations. Retrieved 6-2-2014 from: https://www.davidlynchfoundation.org/research.html)

Lazarus, A. A. et.al. (1976). *Multimodal behavior therapy.* Oxford, England: Springer.

Placebo-effect. (2014) Retrieved March 27, 2014 from: http://psychology.about.com/od /pindex/f/placebo-effect.htm).

Maslow, A. (1968) Toward a psychology of being. New York: Van Nostrand.

Maslow, A. (1954). *Motivation and personality.* New York: Harper.

Meditation (2012). Retrieved June 29, 2012 from: http://medical-dictionary.thefreedictionary.com/meditation

Meditation (2014) The mammalian diving reflex. Retrieved 7-2-2014 from http://www.buddhamind.info/leftside/sumaries/q-a/med-is.htm

Meichenbaum, D. (2007) Stress inoculation training: A preventative and treatment approach. In: P. M. Lehrer, R. L. Woolfolk & W. S. Sime, (Eds.) Principles and practice of stress management (3rd Edition). New York. Guilford.

Meditation-An Introduction (2010) Retrieved June 10, 2014 from: http://nccam.nih. gov/health/meditation/overview.htm

Mowrer, O. H. (1956). Two-factor learning theory reconsidered, with special reference to secondary reinforcement and the concept of habit. PsychologicalReview, 63, 114–128.

Moyers, Bill with Houston Smith (1996) The wisdom of faith. Silver

References

Spring, MD. Athena. DVD, Athenalearning.com.

Murphy, C. (2012). *God's jury: The inquisition and the making of the modern world*. Boston: Houghton, Mifflin, Harcourt.

Naturalism (2012). In Stanford Encyclopedia of Philosophy. Retrieved 3/15/2012. http://plato.stanford.edu/entries/naturalism/

Nirvana (2013) Buddhist Studies. Retrieved July 2, 2013 from: http://www.buddhanet.net/e- learning/dharmadata/fdd43.htm

NPR. (2012, 4/11) To some Hindus, modern yoga has lost its way. *Morning Edition Oberholtzer, J. (2011) Why Benjamin Franklin was more productive than I am.Forbes, April 5, 2011.*

Peaceful Warrior (2006) Lionsgate. Santa Monica, CA

Pew Forum on Religion & Public Life (2008). Washington, DC. U.S. Religious Landscape Survey.

Popper, C. (1959) *The Logic of Scientific Discovery*, translation of Logik der Forschung, London: Hutchinson.

Rogers, Carl (1961). On becoming a person. Boston: Houghton-Mifflin.Russell, B. (1986). God and Religion. Amherst: New York. Prometheus Books.

Schellenberg, J. L. (2007). The wisdom to doubt: A justification of religious skepticism. Ithaca, NY. Cornell University Press.

Segan, Carl (1995) The demon-haunted world: Science as a candle in the dark. New York: Random House.

Shaver, R. (2010) Egoism. *The Stanford Encyclopedia of Philosophy*, Retrieved 4/30/13 from:
    <http://plato.stanford.edu/archives/win2010/entries/egoism/

Socrates-and-his-hemlock (2014) Retrieved April 4, 2014 from http://www.britannica.com/blogs/2009/11/socrates-and-his-hemlock-toxic-tuesdays-a-weekly-guide-to- poison gardens/

Sorensen, S. (2012) Spiritual atheism: The way of wisdom. www.SpiralGarden.com ISBN: 987-0-9858237-1-9

Shepard, G. (1966). In god we trust: All others pay cash. New York, Doubleday.

Spontaneous generation…(2012). Microbial World. Retrieved June

19, 2012. http://www.microbiologytext.com/ Index.php?module=Book&func=displayarticle&art_id=27 Stage of Grief Models: Kubler-Ross (2012). Retrieved November 13, 2012 from: php?type=doc&id=8444&cn=58

Secret Files of the Inquisition (2006) Arlington, VA: PBS

Shook, J. R. Dimeff, L. (2001). Dialectical behavior therapy in a nutshell, The California Psychologist, 34, 10-13.

Shook, J. R. (2006) Varieties of Naturalism. Retrieved October 6, 2012 from: http://www.naturalisms.org/

Smith, Houston (1958) The world's religions. New York: Harper Collins.

Starfish… Regeneration (2012) Retrieved August 13, 2012 from: http://www.susanscott.net/ OceanWatch2001/may25-01.html

Roberti , J. W. (2004) A review of behavioral and biological correlates of sensation seeking. Journal of Research in Personality 38 256–279

The Middle Way. (2013) Retrieved June 24, 2013 from: http://themiddleway.net/?p=230

Thomas, M. (2012). Why Atheism? Retrieved June 6, 2012. http://www.godlessgeeks.com/WhyAtheism.html

Trait theory. (2013) Retrieved June 20, 2013 from: http://psychology.about.com /od/theoriesofpersonality/a/trait-theory.htm

Unitarian Universalism (2012) Retrieved August 11, 2012 from: http://www.religionfact.com/a-z-religion-index/unitarian_universalism.html

US Holocaust Museum, (2013) Niemöller, M. First they came for the Socialist. Retrieved May   7, 2013 from http://www.ushmm .org/wlc/en/article.php?ModuleId=10007392

References

Vyse, S. (2013) Believing in Magic: The Psychology of Superstition. New York: Oxford University Press.

Wallace, A. (2013) Fear of Death: It's About Life, Actually. Let's Talk About It. CreateSpace.Amazon.com

Ware, K. (2013) The Way of the Ascetics: Negative or Affirmative? http://www29 homepage.villanova.edu/christopher.haas/ascetics.html

Watts, A.W. (1957) *The way of Zen*, New York: Vintage.

Weiss, B. (2003) New York: Hay House. Eliminating Stress, Finding Inner Peace.

Whyte, W.H. (1956) The organization man. New York: Simon & Schuster. What Is The Middle Way? (2013) Retrieved June 24, 2013 from: http:// themiddleway.net/?p=230

Wolpe, J. (1958) *Psychotherapy by Reciprocal Inhibition*. Stanford, CA. Stanford University Press.

Wuthnow, R (1998). After heaven: Spirituality in America since the 1950s. Berkeley: University of California Press.

Yalom, I. D. (2008) Staring at the sun: Overcoming the terror of death. San Francisco: Josie-Bass

Life, Death and Spirituality

INDEX

A, B, C Paradigm, 174

Advocacy, 19

American Humanist Association, 96

Archimedes, 22, 24

Audience effect-, 66

Born Good, 8

Breathe Control Relaxation Exercise, 114

Buddhist, 24, 26, 29, 30, 65, 98, 99, 125, 129, 145, 146, 165, 166, 186, 199

Calvin, 6, 194

Check and Shake-Out., 116

Confirmation bias, 67

death, 47

Death Phobia, 46

Demonizing, 67

Do it Yourself, 68

East -West, 34
Epicurus, 62, 70, 71

False "reasoning"-, 67

Fear of the Dark, vii, 49, 50

Free Balance Position, 130

freethinker, 2

General Social Survey, 11

Grit, 103, 105, 106, 162

Hemlock, 89

Human Condition, 44

Humanism, 96, 197

Little Book of Atheist Spirituality, 84

Magic, viii, 91, 103, 106, 107, 189, 201

meditation, 34

Mindfulness, 160, 165, 198

Natural World, 47, 48

Naturalism, 93, 94, 199, 200

Phobia,, 50

Phobias, 53

Rationalism, 94

Relaxation, viii, 111, 112, 114

Religion, 9, 79

Risk, 183
Sacralizeing, 67

SBNG World View, 80

Self-Regulation, 26

Spirituality, 79

SPNG, 19, 184

Subjective Units of Discomfort, 140

Supernatural World, 47, 48

What Should I Do?, 57

ABOUT THE AUTHOR

With more than 35 years practical experience in psychology practice and teaching, I bring a substantial understanding of people's strengths, skills and resources as well as their stressors, fears, and vulnerabilities. These clinical skills, together with a practical commitment to make sense out of my own life converge to inspire this book.

I am now retired from active clinical service, but retain an understanding of, not only personal and clinical problems, but also the genuine angst experienced by people struggling with a religious heritage that does not work for them.

I have published in the areas of professional and ethical issues, interpersonal relationships, and skills and served as an editorial reviewer for a professional psychology journals.

Printed in Great Britain
by Amazon